The Happy Helpful Grandma Guide

by
Leslie Lehr Spirson

with
Claire J. Lehr, Ph.D.

Meadowbrook Press

Distributed by Simon & Schuster

New York

Library of Congress Cataloging-in-Publication Data
Spirson, Leslie Lehr.
    The happy helpful grandma guide / by Leslie Lehr Spirson with Claire J. Lehr.
        p.   cm.
    ISBN 088166-239-9 (pbk.). — ISBN 0-671-53494-7 (pbk.)
    1. Grandmothers—Family relationships. 2. Grandparenting.
I. Lehr, Claire J. II. Title
HQ759.9.S73   1995
306.874'5—dc20   95-33154
                                                                          CIP

Simon & Schuster Ordering # 0-671-53494-7

Editorial Coordinator, Editor: Liya Lev Oertel
Copyeditor: Jean-Marie Sohlden
Production Manager: Amy Unger
Cover Design: Linda Norton

Trade paperback edition published by Meadowbrook Press, 18318 Minnetonka
Boulevard, Deephaven, MN 55391.

BOOK TRADE DISTRIBUTION by Simon & Schuster,
a division of Simon and Schuster, Inc., 1230 Avenue of the Americas,
New York, NY 10020.

99 98 97 96 95   10 9 8 7 6 5 4 3 2 1

Printed in the United States of America

For Juliette & Catherine

To Grandmas Everywhere:
Enjoy the Children!

Contents

1

Introduction

"How old are your grandchildren?"
"Well, the doctor's two and the lawyer's four."
— Anonymous

Congratulations! It's time to reap the rewards of motherhood. Time to feel special and wonderful and beautiful and proud. Time to fall in love again. The work is over — now the fun begins!

Have you been eyeing baby clothes for years? Or did the news take you completely by surprise? Were you shocked at the vision of your son as a father? Did you give not-so-subtle hints to your daughter? Maybe you were looking forward to the announcement, but when it came, you were secretly anxious. You're not alone. In fact, even if you have a closet full of pink and blue Sleep'n Plays, it's natural to be a little bit nervous. After all, grandchildren are living proof that your children are getting older. Luckily, being a grandmother is one of the most rewarding roles you'll ever have.

It takes years to grow from infancy to adulthood to parenthood. No matter how many years lie between, you've still got the majority of your life left — as a grandmother. For the first time in history, women can enjoy an average of forty years of grandparenting. Just when you're feeling the mid-life blahs, a precious gift is given to you — a baby to love, spoil, and then give back to the parents!

You can't choose to be a grandmother. You can, however, choose what kind of grandmother to be. Suddenly, those nine long months are up, and you are biologically connected to a brand new person. As a grandparent, you can explore the world from a fresh perspective, nurture and influence the future, and enjoy a wonderful relationship with a child who wants to love you forever. You can make a difference in your grandchildren's lives — and you can have fun doing it! Take advantage of the happiness ahead. Learn how to be a "great" grandma.

You know you're a grandma when ...

— the clerk at the toy store knows you by name.

— your children ask you for advice.

— you realize that "Rock A Bye Baby" is not a nice song.

— you think it's adorable when young children are on the answering machine message.

2

Becoming a Grandmother

Perfect love sometimes does not come
until the first grandchild.
— Welsh proverb

The First Grandchild

You'll always remember exactly where you were when you first became a grandmother. I know my mother will — she was with me. The awe of creation ignited a rebirth of our relationship. We shared an unforgettable experience from two very different points of view.

Grandma's Story

The call came first thing in the morning. My son-in-law said, "You're going to be a grandmother — soon!" Chills went down my spine. "Are you serious? How is she? Oh my God, I've got to pack!"

I rushed around throwing my things into an overnight bag. It was ten days before she was due. I wasn't ready. The hospital was in Santa Monica — I lived in Orange County, an hour and a half away.

I rushed inside St. John's Hospital. I was so proud, I announced to everyone I saw that my daughter was having a baby. As I turned the corner of the maternity ward, I saw Leslie pacing the corridor with that huge baby in her belly. Jon was helping her. Leslie saw me. With tears in her eyes, she looked like the baby she had been, years ago. I was elated and frightened all at once. This was it. Real Life.

The birthing room was scary — like a normal hotel room but with tubes and monitors all over the place. It reminded me of Star Trek. The parents-to-be had brought lots of cassette tapes. I have absolutely no idea what music I heard, even though it played all day and most of the night. At one point we turned on the television and watched bits of All My Children. Leslie was in a lot of pain. I don't know why they didn't give her more medication; I didn't like that natural childbirth stuff. When I gave birth to her, the nurse knocked me right out — it was civilized. To distract everyone, I pulled out a new book of short stories and started reading out loud. I felt like part of the coaching team. I could barely read through my tears.

My son-in-law announced that if it was a girl, her middle name would be Claire, for me. I said, "It doesn't matter if it's a girl or a boy, as long as it's healthy." But I couldn't help it. I was seduced. I wanted a girl.

Finally, early the next morning, it was time. Worn out, I left the special event to the Spirson team. A few minutes later, I heard a baby cry. They invited me back in and I saw her. Juliette Claire was the most incredible baby in all the world. I was part of it all. And she was part of me.

My Story

I waited as long as I could before letting my husband call my mother. I was excited to have her there, yet I felt possessive about the experience, wanting it to belong only to us.

I didn't mean to cry — I didn't want to cry — but when I saw my mother, I just couldn't help it. I was so relieved she had made it. Like many mothers and daughters, we've had a rocky relationship, but now we had motherhood in common. The next contraction reminded me that she went through all this pain for me once. I was grateful.

My mother badgered the nurses so much I would have been embarrassed if I hadn't been in so much pain. I was self-conscious about asking for drugs so I waited until I couldn't stand it. By then, all the shot did was make a red dot on my bottom. They wouldn't give me the epidural until I was farther along. My husband was watching the monitor and tried to pacify me once by saying the contraction was only a mild one, but the monitor lied and I let him know it. Mom watched cheerfully and made small talk, but she was as nervous as she was at my wedding. I felt like a wild animal thrashing about.

At some point, Mom pulled out a book and started reading short stories. I thought she was out of her mind ... then the stories got interesting. She had to start over when contractions interrupted, but it turned out to be a wonderful distraction.

We had decided on a girl's first name but that was about it. It's amazing that you have all those months to pick names and it's still so impossible. My husband blurted out that we would name a girl Juliette Claire, with the middle name after my mother. We hadn't agreed on this, but he pretty much ended the discussion right there. I wasn't up to an argument, and we couldn't exactly take it back. My Mom was so overjoyed, you'd think it never crossed her mind. I realized it was a good thing — this baby would never be lacking in the grandma department.

Natural Reactions to the News

Q: What do you say when you hear the news?
A: I'm going to be a matriarch!

No matter what your immediate thoughts are about becoming a grandmother, once the reality sinks in, instinct takes over. Your baby is going to have a baby. Seems like yesterday, you were the one changing diapers.

Reminiscing

The first thing my mother did was typical of all new grandmothers: she dug out the family scrapbook and bored everyone who dared step foot in her home. Then she started sending me faded old photographs in the mail. Did this prove that I was cute or just that she really was a mother, way back when? Either way, now I have dozens of ancient pictures shoved in my albums at random, and she has a book with a lot of empty, faded squares. It was a natural response, though, so I tried to be understanding.

Your children will try to be understanding, too ... until you start sending child development books by the caseload. In a few short weeks I amassed a full library of baby books, child psychology tomes, and medical texts. Suddenly, I had subscriptions to half a dozen parenting magazines. My mother also sent nursery rhyme anthologies, in case I forgot. She even threw in a children's dictionary, for future reference. Finally, when it was time for a new bookcase, I called her on the phone.

"So, Mom, hey, thanks for the books."

"Oh, did you get them?" She sounded nonchalant.

"I sure did. All of them. I mean, I hope it's all of them. The UPS man swears whenever he sees me. He's getting a hernia."

"That's crude, honey."

"Sorry. So, tell me the truth . . . you don't think I'll be a good mother?"

That did it. The dam broke. She sobbed. "That's not it. I just never taught you how!"

"It's not like there's a test, Mom. So far as I know, they just hand you the baby in the hospital, no license or anything."

"Well, there should be something. It's the most important thing you'll ever do. You didn't even like to baby-sit!"

"That's because our neighbors' daughter was a brat."

"I just want you to be prepared. It's a big job, you know."

"I know, Mom, but I can always call you for help, right?"

Your concern is natural. Give your children as much information as possible. Then trust biology for that maternal instinct to kick in. And keep an open telephone line!

Connecting the Past with the Future

Suddenly, I was being regaled with stories about my great-grandparents. I know Mom was enjoying her ride down memory lane, and it was pretty interesting, so I just listened. After a few weeks, I realized she was savoring memories as a method of gathering research. She was building a model of The Perfect Grandma in her mind. We're talking half a century ago, and somehow I knew my mother would never grow her hair to the floor and wear it wrapped up in a braid. Hey, she's a California blonde! I also knew she wouldn't be luring the children to the kitchen with the aroma of fresh-baked sweets. I was confident that she'd keep a cupboard full of Cheerios and hit the Chinese take-out place regularly.

Then she started collecting family histories. With a psychotherapist for a mother, I'm used to having my family and friends dissected on a regular basis. But now she wasn't just fooling around with idle research. She was examining patterns of parenting to see how my husband and I would stack up. It was scary.

Next she started planning the financial strategy necessary to buy her grandchild a pony and take her on sightseeing trips around the world. She also took seminars on college tuition planning. Unless she won the lottery, most of these plans were a bit unrealistic, but it was the thought that counted.

During my pregnancy, mom's favorite activity was playing the name game. Everywhere she went, my mother asked people their full names. She watched the credits roll on every movie and television show and took notes in case she found the perfect name. She called me whenever she heard a new one. This was fun for a while, but there came the time when I was ready to call the kid Bozo the Clown just to end the discussion.

Mom's enthusiasm was starting to wear on me. I mean, I was excited, but I also had heartburn, varicose veins, bags under my eyes, and an embarrassingly weak bladder. She was happy, healthy, and wild with anticipation. She would tell me about the new baby store in her neighborhood before mentioning that her credit card was stolen. Overwhelming excitement is natural, and it doesn't go away — not for the second grandchild or the third, or even, as many grandmothers have told me, the fifteenth. Each baby is another jewel in your crown.

Knowing that your bloodline will extend into the future brings a sense of immortality—and pride. After all, what the world really needs is more of you, right? A woman's eggs are formed while she is a fetus in her mother's belly. So, if you have a daughter, her children are definitely made of your stuff. Your imprint will be on this Earth for decades, if not centuries, to come. Immortality is even more clear when the family name — as well as your blood — lives on.

It's not just blood, however, that determines ancestry. If your children or grandchildren are adopted, your influence has profound significance. Your grandchildren may pick up your sense of humor or your loyalty or your zest for life. They will certainly blossom from your spiritual gifts and, in turn, they will pass them on to the next generation. Grandchildren are a magic potion that lets you live forever.

The Baby Shower

The importance of this event cannot be stressed too much. Sure, a baby shower is an excuse to get presents, but more than that, it's a show of support. If the new mother's friends haven't made solid plans by the fifth month, step right up! The baby shower can be a potluck picnic, a formal tea, or a buffet brunch. It can be in your home, at a restaurant, or at the guest-of-honor's house. If need be, you can plan it from across the country: request a list of names and addresses, mail the invitations, pick up party supplies, and be there a day ahead to prepare.

When I had my first baby, I didn't know any other mothers, so my mother and I held our own shower. Mom cooked her delicious seafood casserole, I made Chinese chicken salad, and my sister flew down in time to ball honeydew into a scooped-out watermelon. My husband helped decorate, then escaped to the movies. It was an awful lot of work, and we probably could have bought all the gifts ourselves just as easily. Nevertheless, planning the shower was fun and it meant a lot to my mother and sister and me at the start of a newly defined, post-baby relationship.

By the time my second child made her appearance, several of my new "Mommy" friends pitched in to share a babysitter, and my mother was simply another name on the guest list. I was pretty laid back about this party — we even waited until the baby was born to ascertain my need for baby clothes. Mostly I just wanted to show the baby off. My sister was flying down to represent the family, and I didn't really care if my mother made the hour-and-a-half drive up. Or so I thought.

When the big day came, my mother called and asked if it mattered whether she came. She was tired and the drive was a pain and we'd seen her a lot in the past month. I said I didn't mind, and at that moment I believed it. Then I hung up. Suddenly, I couldn't believe she didn't care enough to come to her own daughter's baby shower. I was devastated. I picked up the phone a dozen times to call her back , but pride made me hang up. Then I got angry. If she didn't want to be there, then it must not be important. What did it matter? Why should I care? Besides, I still had to shower and nurse the baby and put on mascara for the first time in weeks. I threw myself into the task. By the time I had my dress on, there was a knock on the door. She must have driven at the speed of light! I was so happy to see her I cried through my mascara and had redo my eyes all over again.

A baby shower is similar to a christening or a bris: it's a rite of passage for the new family. If your daughter-in-law is having the baby, your participation is even more important. Since bonding with her may not be your natural inclination, it will mean a great deal more in the long run. By having the shower, you might forge a real relationship between the two of you. If someone else has the shower, your enthusiastic attendance will reflect your good intentions and help you become friends in the interest of the baby.

Some baby showers are thrown as couples parties — barbecues, brunches, or even cocktail soirees. If your son is the new father, having the men present may make participation easier. Take advantage of this opportunity. Be on the welcome wagon for your grandchild. Sharing these happy events will build a lasting bond with the expanding family.

How to Help during Labor
Your Daughter

If you are interested in being there during labor, discuss the possibilities with your daughter. In all the excitement, she may not have thought about it. Assure her that you'll do whatever makes her feel the most comfortable. Let your desires be known, then follow hers.

If you are invited, go; don't be afraid to do so. Find out if your daughter plans on natural childbirth; it would be hard to see your child in pain. In any case, attending the birth of your grandchild will be an experience you will never forget.

Reminisce about your own delivery without making light of hers. Tell jokes, tell stories, tell the nurses to bring ice chips! Remember, any distraction is a good distraction.

If you can't be there, be in touch. Send flowers immediately. Mail her a copy of the New York Times or the Los Angeles Times printed on the baby's birthday to save for posterity. Better yet, send a new bathrobe or a casual outfit appropriate for the jubilant trek home from the hospital. By the end of nine months, most new mothers are as anxious for a change of clothes as they are to have that baby! When shopping, think cheerful, loose, and easy access for breastfeeding.

Your Daughter-in-Law

If your daughter-in-law asks you to be present in the delivery room, and if you feel comfortable being there, go right ahead. Otherwise, wait to visit until after the baby is born. My friend's mother-in-law was allowed in the labor and delivery room by the friendly hospital staff. Vicky loves her mother-in-law, but she would have appreciated some privacy. If you recall, childbirth is a very messy ordeal. Vicky was embarrassed and felt she deserved more respect. More importantly, she wanted her husband all to herself. After so much effort, she needed some personal attention.

Your daughter-in-law doesn't want to make waves. So you should test the water before you jump in. Once the baby is born, you can ingratiate yourself into the household best by making things as easy as possible for the parents. Cook dinner, hire maid service, entertain the other children, or watch the baby so the parents can take a much-needed nap. The new parents will appreciate and value anything you do for them.

If you cannot be with the new parents soon after delivery, call often. Keep the conversation brief. Send a gift that will stand out from the crowd: his-and-hers slippers (for nighttime feedings), a roll of film, a lullaby tape, a petit point baby announcement, or a personalized baby blanket. Being far away doesn't take any of the glamour from grandmotherhood — for you or the children. You're special wherever you are.

Your Baby's Baby

The greatest bond is between mother and child. There is no more touching picture than a woman with her newborn. A father rounds out the portrait nicely. However, most women say that even in such an ideal circumstance, something is missing from the picture: they experience an emotional emptiness, a desire for their own mother to be there.

In fact, many new parents' biggest disappointment after childbirth is that their mothers aren't there to share the spectacle of new life and complete the circle. During the birth of my younger child, my mother was busy caring for my oldest. I knew she would have loved to be with me, yet I still felt that empty space.

If you can, be there for your baby. Be there for your baby's baby. Be there for you. Grandchildren are the second greatest bond.

Bonding

Do you believe in love at first sight? It's a common phenomenon with grandbabies. The first cry makes you appreciate the miracle of creation. The first look jump-starts your heart into a lifelong love affair. When I first mentioned "bonding" to my husband, he asked if it was anything like Bondo, the glue. I had to laugh but, actually, it is. Once you're smitten, you're pretty well stuck. That's why seeing the baby is vital: visual imprinting makes a difference! The more time you spend with your grandchild early on, the closer you'll feel to that child as he or she grows up — when compared with grandchildren you saw less often.

A word of warning before you rush to the hospital to hold the newborn: beware of Mommy's possessiveness. Breastfeeding guarantees a certain amount of intimacy, but that might not be enough. For some reason, I expected my mother to help out with the new baby by helping out with the house: you know, the laundry, the meals — the yucky stuff. After one load of laundry, she made her intentions clear. It was the baby she wanted and the baby she'd have. I had to bribe her to give the baby back! We teased her and called her "the Grandma from Hell." She didn't care what we said as long as she got to hold the baby. The image of her moving the baby out of my reach makes me laugh even now. The fact is, neither of us had realized how much we wanted the baby to ourselves. So, be forewarned: wait your turn for the baby. Soon, the new mother will be only too happy to let you soothe that baby indefinitely. "Okay, Mom, your turn now ... please!"

If you are unable to meet the baby right away or to stay for any amount of time, you have many other ways to bond with your new grandchild. Put a big photograph of you (holding the baby, ideally) near the bassinet or the changing table. Babies love faces — yours will become familiar and welcome. Plastic key rings are a popular infant toy, and at least one brand includes indestructible photo frames. Such a key ring is the perfect gift for a teething infant, and it helps develop tactile skills. Recognizing your picture and those of others she loves will be a bonus. Also, you can address the olfactory sense by sending a scarf or comfort blanket with your scent. Wear it, sleep with it, add a dash of your perfume, and the baby will know whenever you are near. Another fun way to bond is through sound. Send an audio tape of your favorite lullaby for baby to listen to at bedtime; on the flip side, record nursery rhymes for playtime. Sing those tunes on the telephone and in person, and you'll be regarded as the special friend you are — grandma.

Grandma Names around the World

What do you want to be called? Pick a name — any name — and stick with it. Many silly sounding nicknames are simplifications so the baby can say it easily — and earlier. Some are actually derivatives from other languages. Around the world, "grandma" sounds like this:

Afrikaans: Ouma
Arabic: Sitt, Jadda-t
Bulgarian: Baba
Chinese: Zu-mu
Danish: Bedstemoder
Dutch: Oma, Grootmoeder
English: Grandmother, Grandma, Gramma, Granny, Nanny
Eskimo: Ananatsiark
Finnish: Isoäiti, Mummo
French: Grandmère, Grandmaman
German: Grossmutter, Oma
Greek: Yiayia
Hawaiian: Kupua wahine, Tutu
Hebrew: Savta
Hungarian: Nagyanya

Irish: Nana, Seanamhair
Italian: Nonna
Japanese: Obaa-San
Korean: Hal-mō-ni
Norwegian: Bestemor
Polish: Babka
Portuguese: Avó
Romanian: Buinaita
Russian: Babushka
Spanish: Abuela, Abuelita
Swahili: Nyanya
Swedish: Mormor
Turkish: Büyük anne
Vietnamese: Bà
Welsh: Mamgu, Nain
Yiddish: Bobbeh
Zulu: Gogo

Any name will work. It doesn't matter what they call you ... as long as they call you, right?

You know you're a grandma when ...

— the man of your dreams is six years old.

— your phone bill would pay off the national debt.

— you know the difference between Bert and Ernie.

— you immediately see a family resemblance in that squalling newborn's face.

— you send the grandchildren home.

3

Benefits of
Being a Grandma

Spoil them, love them, indulge them, then send them
back to their parents to civilize them again.
— Joan McIntosh, American writer

Raising children is as tough as it is rewarding. You will always be a mother. But being a grandmother is a lot more fun. In fact it's both revenge and reward.

Yesterday, as I was being fitted for new reading glasses, I mentioned to the optometrist that I needed a sturdy frame to withstand the yanking of tiny hands. That comment opened the floodgate. The woman exclaimed, "Oh my goodness, I love being a grandma! This weekend my granddaughter stayed at our house and slept with us. She kicked a lot, but I didn't care. It was so much fun, all that kissing and giggling. We gave her ice cream for dinner and let her stay up late."

"Sounds like fun," I said.

"I especially love not having to discipline her," she added. "That's not my job."

"Oh, Grandpa does that?" I asked.

"No, no, her parents do that. Our job is to spoil her and give her back. Best job I ever had," she declared.

All this, completely unbidden. I doubt I can write off my doctor's appointment in the name of research, but it does show how universal this joyful act of grandparenting really is.

Here are some of the fun benefits for members of Club Grandma.

A Special Friendship

Forget rules and routines. Kids want to have fun — and you're the person to share it with. Your unique position in the family attracts natural adoration from the grandchildren. After all, you love them no matter what, no expectations or requirements. They've passed the test by being born. Your situation is ideal for becoming best friends and confidants. They can confide in you because they expect emotional support rather than rationality and behavior lessons.

My three-year-old daughter told me she got a small burn on her hand because the window bit her. Obviously, she wished that was the truth. However, she admitted to her grandmother that her hand touched the toaster when she put the bread in. She knew I would have given her a stern reminder that she was not to use the toaster by herself, nor stand on a chair to reach it. But Grandma Claire wasn't obligated to do anything but comfort her.

As a grandma, you are a friend with special power. You are a friend who can make toast. Better yet, you are a friend who can reach the cookie jar!

The Dress-up Game

Juliette loves to primp for Grandma Claire. And, I dare say, my mother makes a special effort as well, often dressing in bright colors and fun accesories. Enjoy dressing up for somebody who truly appreciates your essence! No need to throw away that Mickey Mouse watch — your grandchildren will love seeing it on you. Keep those wardrobe cast-offs for dress-up. Clothes and accessories have a new life with grandchildren.

The True You

Children don't care what you do in the real world. Oh sure, teenagers might be impressed that you're a Supreme Court justice, but mostly they'll appreciate you for being yourself. You can relax and enjoy yourself with these people who love you mainly because you exist. You can drop the outside roles and pretenses. My daughter and mother enjoy pretending they are each other: Grandma Claire will be Juliette for a few hours, and vice versa. It gets confusing sometimes, but I know Juliette must love Grandma Claire a lot if she so enjoys being her.

If you value yourself, the children will value you as well. In turn, you'll value yourself more and realize, after all this time, who you truly are.

Personal Freedom

Contrary to popular belief, close family relationships create independent individuals, whether they are six or sixty. The emotional support acts as a secure base from which you can leap into the world and fly. With this security, you'll find yourself more self-reliant, more active, and more social than ever before. No longer are you defined by your work or marital status: you are a grandma, a well-loved and respected member of society. You are free to do whatever makes you happy.

Taking the Good Times with You

Since you are not constantly in attendance, "photograph" the happy moments with your grandchildren in your mind. You can ignore negative situations by creating a happy memory to remember them by. Let's say your birthday picnic was rained out, your son and his wife fought all day, and your granddaughter had a noisy tantrum. Recapture that exquisite moment when she helped you blow out the candles then hugged you with all her might. Later, take that picture out and enjoy those warm fuzzy feelings again. When someone asks how your birthday was, you can say it was wonderful.

V.I.P.

Everything you do is special, by definition. So you can teach your way of doing things. Not bad things, just the usual things — but your way. A little power goes a long way. Setting the table, making the bed — there are many different methods for even ordinary tasks. You can let your grandchildren in on a special technique and chuckle when you hear them tell their parents they want to do it grandma's way.

Keep in mind that fun with you encompasses a wide range of activities. Something described as a "chore" at home or "work" at school can be "fun" with you. Teaching your grandchild how to write thank-you notes falls well within the fun category as long as it is an activity shared with you. Grandma's smile is infectious.

The Sky's the Limit

Learn new skills without embarrassment. So you've never quite caught up to the computer age? No problem. Your grandchildren will be thrilled to teach you. They get to show off and be the experts — you get to learn without pressure. In return, you can visit the putting range together and teach them how to play golf.

A Bridge to Your Children

Grandchildren will bring you and your child closer. Your children may be grown, but this is the first time you can truly enjoy an adult relationship with them. In the world of parenting, you are now peers. Once I became a mother, I definitely saw my own mother in a different light — one of respect and, yes, appreciation. I can still feel angry with her now and then, but it's different. We can relate. We're friends. I actually call her now — for advice or just to chat.

Living Longer

Grandparents live longer. Have you heard the statistics that show married men live longer than unmarried men, because they are loved and taken care of? Do you know a couple who passed away within weeks of each other? Human contact is vital to us all. We live for love.

My mother-in-law was ailing when we met. My husband and I were married three years before our first child was born, but she hung in there. When Juliette was eight weeks old, we flew up to Seattle to introduce them. I'll never forget the joy on Grandma Jean's face when she held that baby. What was she thinking when she looked into Juliette's eyes? Immortality? Completing the circle of life? That night Grandma Jean was put in the hospital and we spent the next day visiting her there. She held the baby and chuckled a lot. Her eyes were sparkling — she was strong and full of life. Weeks later, she passed away. She is with us always, not only in our hearts but also in a photograph of our visit that hangs on the wall. Juliette loves to look at that picture.

Until you experience your grandchild, you have not yet experienced everything, and this experience is worth the wait. Love is everything.

Spirituality

Now that you are connected with the future, doesn't every little thing seem related to one grand scheme of things? Whether or not you practice a formal religion, the existence of some higher power is likely to be in your thoughts. You have experienced the essence of nature itself.

Many grandparents initiate the habit of bedtime prayers. It can be the start of a spiritual bond between you and the forces that brought you and your grandchild together. No other time may seem as peaceful as when your grandchild says her prayers and you tuck her safely in bed. It establishes a very special relationship between the two of you.

You know you're a grandma when ...

— you don't mind being drooled on.

— you buy an expensive miniature party dress that will be outgrown in three months.

— you hang up the phone and realize you forgot to talk to your son.

— you believe coloring on the walls demonstrates creativity.

— you get a special feeling that never goes away.

4

Tips for New Grandmas

The quickest way to be convinced that spanking is unnecessary is to become a grandparent.
— Anonymous

Being a grandmother will not take over your whole life — and it shouldn't! It will, however, change your outlook on life while adding a rich new dimension to it. Here are some inside tips to ease the transition to this exciting new aspect of your life.

Help Should be Helpful

Beware of being invasive. The new parents could consider your unsolicited advice meddlesome, helpful as it might be. This is tricky, because when your child calls you with a problem, you might think she is looking for a solution. However, that might not be the case.

Unless she specifically asks for suggestions, assume that she wants you to listen, acknowledge her feelings, and be understanding.

Be careful even in simple situations: if you make lunch for the kids, find out what their parents want them to eat. If you really want to help, check with Mom and Dad first. When it comes to advice, less is more. A word of experience from you can speak volumes to one who is listening.

Scrapbook Time

Now is your chance to coo over pictures of your son in his sailor suit. Children love to see their parents as youngsters. Comparing looks and behavior helps them understand growing up, lets them poke harmless fun at their parents, and allows you all to have a great time.

"I Am Not Your Grandma"

Your grandchildren's name for you represents your family's emotional relationship. This name is personal and nobody else should use it. My mother was dating a man who called her "Grams" once. Although my mother loves being a grandma and she doesn't hide the crib in her living room, it was their last date. The use of the glorious title "grandma" is reserved for a special few.

Fountain of Youth

Being a grandma is the best excuse to be a kid again. Although your grandchildren might guess that you're one hundred, they have no concept of what that really means. To the contrary, they will naturally assume you have the same preposterous amount of energy that they do!

Kids love to play games — any games. From peek-a-boo to charades, games keep everybody on their toes. (They also teach valuable communication and relationship skills.)

Poetry often describes youth as the age of wonder. So shed your preconceptions and join your grandchildren in staring at the clouds. Explore every leaf and twig on a tour around the same old block. Get reacquainted with the child in you. Children make you young at heart.

Open House

Leave out your welcome mat and you'll always be welcome at your grandchildren's house. When the children feel comfortable in your environment, they'll want you to share their own turf. Public relations experts stress that participation equals belonging. Be part of the family. Help yourself to a glass of juice and allow them to do the same at your house.

In some situations, like a nursing home or even a second marriage, the concept of "grandma's house" might not be realistic. Do whatever you feel comfortable with. Remember, the children are after your heart, not your home.

If you live close enough to your children, the open door policy will keep you warm through the winter. Parents want to keep their children happy. If that means going to your house or inviting you over, make the visit attractive to them. It helps to always call before you want to drop in. Ask that they always check with you, as well. Face it, sometimes we're just not up to seeing people, even those we love. *Respect each other's privacy, and you'll enjoy more time together.*

If you live far away, extend a blanket invitation to the family, with the condition of checking your schedule first. Ask when a good time to visit their house would be and stress that they needn't clear the decks to entertain you. To really get to know the children, join them in their regular activities: take them to the park, watch a martial arts class, or enjoy their reactions to the latest sing-along video. Bring your own entertainment — books, crocheting, movie money, or walking shoes — to fill in the time. Offer to baby-sit so the parents can have dinner out. Beware, they may want to keep you!

Indispensable You

You are the best baby nurse, the best sitter, and the best party helper because you have a vested interest. In an emergency, would you rather have your children call a stranger? If your grandchild has a problem he is afraid to ask Mommy about, wouldn't you like for him to call you? You can be the heroine in times of need.

Be a part of the family even when you live far away. Give the baby a toy phone to play with, then call up and speak with him over the real one. As a birthday present, give a cuddly night-night doll so the child remembers you. Buy two copies of your favorite bedtime book, send one copy to your grandchild, and read in tandem over the phone on Sunday nights, when the rates are low. Record yourself singing lullabies to soothe the baby to sleep. Become part of the day-to-day reality of your grandchildren, and they'll also become a part of yours.

You Are Not Alone

Some of you are raising your grandchildren, perhaps by yourself. To enrich the special relationship between you and your grandchild, utilize the many existing support systems. Local organizations are available to help. Look to the elementary school system, adult education programs at the community college, and area churches and synagogues for special programs aimed at you. Many hospitals and birthing programs offer "Mommy and Me" classes that welcome grandmothers with open arms. You can also form informal play groups through word of mouth or with the help of a friendly pediatrician. Private support groups are springing up under the domain of family therapists: my mother's therapy group for menopausal women often deals with the joys and challenges of being a grandparent.

Additionally, a growing number of grandparents are involved in such programs as Gymboree and other commercial activity classes for children. Organizations such as the Young Grandparents Club (where "Young" is a state of mind) are listed in national parenting magazines and are forming groups nationwide. If your town has a local parents' newspaper, read it. In fact, read everything you can find. The other day, I noticed a column for grandparents in a union newsletter. Other grandmothers are out there — take a stroll to the neighborhood park and you'll see. Practice pick-up lines such as "How many grandchildren do you have?" and "How old is the baby?" You're not alone. In fact, you'll never be alone again!

Assertiveness Training

The line "I love you but the answer is no" works for grandparents as well as parents. But although you know how to deal with the little ones, the big ones can also make problems by taking you for granted. Tell them no, you can't baby-sit next weekend, you've already made plans. If you'll be honest when you want time for yourself, you'll never resent the time that you do spend with your grandchildren.

Grandma Claire is very specific about her schedule. So, when we are together, I know she's happy about spending time with us. In return, when she wants to stay over an extra night, I can tell her I'd rather have some family time alone.

If you don't feel like listening to your daughter's problems right now, tell her. You'll be more help when you are in the mood. The first time I called my mother in the middle of Barbara Walters, she said she'd call me back, then hung up on me, which was a bit upsetting. Now, I realize this practice saves me from repeating myself when she's not paying attention. Encourage your children to be honest about sharing their time. When you can say no, yes becomes a joy for everyone.

Sleep: A Precious Commodity

For parents of young children, spending the weekend with grandma means sleeping late (eight o'clock, at least!). You don't always have to take the early shift, but when you do, the parents will be incredibly grateful for the rest of the day. Meanwhile, you'll start your day with the people who most adore you. Most children are at their best in the morning, happy and raring to go.

Our youngest daughter, Catherine, has a solar-sensitive cell — if the sun is up, so is she. We've tried everything, from putting her to bed late to blocking out the windows — nothing works. Grandma Claire made up a game to make the early morning hours more fun. When the baby's awake and making sounds, Grandma Claire stands by the crib, puts out her arms, and repeats her own name over and over; but she won't pick her up until Catherine says grandma's name. Something that sounds like it, anyway. Of course, Grandma didn't refuse Catherine when she got frustrated the first few times, but Catherine was a quick study. "I love to hear her call "'Nana,'" my mother told me. "So despite the early hour, I start the day with a thrill."

Feeding and dressing children are time-consuming activities, and you can probably spend the morning watching Sesame Street or Bugs Bunny. If this effort wears you out, nap with the younger ones later.

Your grandchildren won't always be little. Besides, you can catch those extra forty winks tomorrow!

Routine Fun

Wouldn't you like to know when you'll see your grandchildren again? Even if you live close by, seeing them regularly can be difficult — life gets in the way. Solve this problem by adding yourself to their calendar. If you see each other every month, you can create a tradition of taking the child to lunch, for a stroll, to the library, or to the petting zoo. Perhaps you could finish off the day with a bath and a bedtime story.

If you are lucky enough to see them more often than one or two times a month, become a part of the permanent schedule. You could take the baby to a weekly "Baby and Me" class. You could be the chauffeur for the older child's dance classes or swimming lessons. You could host dinner or baby-sit every Thursday. You could assign one morning a week to the preschoolers and plan crafts projects or field trips. The possibilities are endless. After you decide what you would enjoy doing most and find out what works best for everyone, write your name on the family calendar in permanent ink..

Every Day Can Be Special

The best advice for any grandma is to insinuate yourself into the day-to-day life of your grandchildren, even if you live 3,000 miles away. Simply turn ordinary days into exciting events.

You can make the first day of school into a momentous event in your relationship. Grandma Claire spoke with Juliette about her first day of preschool for weeks beforehand. During one visit they counted down to it, marked days off the calendar, and played school with Juliette as the teacher. She sent Juliette a good luck card in the mail, then called her the night before to share her anticipation and ease her concern. Then, after school, she called to see how the big day went. Now, when Juliette remembers the first day of school, she thinks of her grandma as part of the important day."

We all need to avoid putting pressure on children with our expectations of performing well. Just encourage a happy experience. Don't highlight events that are too far in the future. Celebrating a half-birthday, the birthday of the family pet, or even the start of hockey season can bring you closer to an older child, from close or far away.

Create an occasion out of thin air by setting a date during your next visit to watch soccer practice or to see a new movie. Any occasion with you will be a special one.

You know you're a grandma when ...

— you spend an entire day with your daughter-in-law.

— the baby cries in the middle of the night and you don't have to get up.

— you hear "Grandma!" and realize someone's talking to you.

— animal crackers are a staple of your grocery list.

5

Your
Many Roles

Grandparents don't have to be smart — only answer questions
like why dogs hate cats and how come God isn't married.
— Patsy Gray, age nine

Grandmas are more than just fun and games: your importance can't
be overstated. However, with the demise of the extended family, surrogates have taken over many traditional grandmother activities. For
example: fast-food often replaces home cooking; family therapists
help with family problems; celebrities are heroes; television offers
stereotypes of aging; and movies provide a sense of history.
Unfortunately, these surrogates aren't madly in love with the children
as you are. Caring and active grandmas can do all of the above — and
do them much better.

Typically, parents are the most powerful people in a child's universe. One parent typically means playtime: the other parent means business. However, you are a far superior being: a parent's boss. When my mother reminds my daughter that I was in her tummy long ago, that little girl's eyes grow wide. It helps her understand that grandma was there first and that older people are individuals worthy of respect.

Respect works both ways: don't forget to treat the children with respect. Acknowledge a child's feelings whether or not those feelings are justified. A child cannot help what he feels and is therefore especially vulnerable. Once you let him know you understand he is angry or sad, you can address his behavior. In turn, he will learn to respect your feelings.

Children of all ages learn from you to respect the elderly, no matter how old you are. Don't be insulted at being considered "old": teach them that older people can be "with it" and wise at the same time. This is especially relevant for teenagers, whom adults rarely treat as important people. Be sure to let your teenaged grandchildren know you respect them. Relate to each as an individual. Soon you'll have a real friendship.

Remember, your influence is overwhelming. You may think everything you say goes in one ear and out the other, but the strangest thing happens in the middle — your words are burned into memory! Consequently, be gentle. In regular discussions with the children, be careful that your influence is positive.

Following are some of the vital roles you can play in the lives of your grandchildren.

Protector

Who can protect those precious children from the cold, cruel world? You. Kids know they can count on Grandma. Protection can be as simple as insisting on a nap — you are actually protecting them from fatigue. Making your children feel safe can also be complicated, as when World War III erupts in their own home. Then, you can comfort them over the telephone, remove them temporarily from the situation, and give them emotional support.

When you are with your grandchildren, you protect them from strangers as well as hurt feelings. If they're embarrassed to tell Daddy about the school-yard bully, you can take the matter into your own capable hands by talking it through with the child and discussing the situation with Daddy yourself.

When Juliette was twenty months old, Grandma Claire took her to the park near her house. A four-year-old girl grabbed Juliette's shovel and refused to give it back. Juliette immediately looked over to the bench where my mother was sitting and cried out, "Nana!"

Needless to say, Juliette got her shovel back in a jiffy. Both Grandma Claire and Juliette were very pleased about the whole incident. Super Grandma to the rescue!

Teacher

You don't need a degree in early childhood education to be a great teacher to your grandchild. Everything you do serves as an example of good conduct, starting with the basics. As a baby, your grandchild will copy the sound you make when you click your tongue. Try it! She'll blow kisses after seeing you blow them to her. She'll learn to talk by repeating your words.

Later on, things get a little more complicated. She will continue to learn by mimicking behavior — not just her parents' actions, but yours as well. She will unconsciously begin to think along the same lines. Ethics and values, the most vital elements of a person's behavior throughout their life, are learned early, and you are an excellent source for them. Be good!

You are also the best history teacher they'll ever have. Children love stories. Tales of your experience in the real world teach them about that world in a direct, nonthreatening manner. My grandfather was a young child when his family escaped from Russia in 1917. Visions of the family jewels sewn into his jacket as his sled was pulled over the snow during that midnight escape make the Bolshevik Revolution come alive for me. Stories told by my grandmother about my great-grandfather's promotion of Gypsy Rose Lee have made the vaudeville era a reality as well. Your life is more glamorous than you might think, so describe it in terms of the big picture, adding details to make it personal. Did you collect tin cans after World War II? My mother remembers stepping on them to make them flat and easier to handle. Did you wear love beads during the sixties? Grandma Claire wore a medallion that read, "War is unhealthy for children and other living things." Make history come alive for your grandchildren. Teach them well.

Role Model
For Granddaughters

To your granddaughter, you are the prime example of what a mature woman should be. Although she gets the basics from her mother, that relationship is fraught with other concerns. At times she will be prone to rebel from being cast in her mother's shadow. You are the archetype. Help her standards be high.

For Grandsons

Have you ever heard the claim that the way a man treats his mother is a precursor of the way he'll treat his wife? Let's take this theory a little farther: if your grandson respects and values you, he is likely to do the same with other mature women. Your part is simply to be a good role model, so give him an example as reference. When you hear how he helped a woman pick up the groceries that fell out of her bag, give yourself a pat on the back.

Caregiver

Where did this term "caregiver" come from, anyway? My guess is that it's a politically correct combination of caretaker, nanny, helper, friend, housekeeper, babysitter, surrogate Mommy — in short: Grandma! If you live close enough, you can be your family's favorite caregiver.

Forget daycare, television, and babysitters: you are the real thing. If you are able to offer any time to your grandchildren, be assertive. Since your children consider baby-sitting a job (and justifiably so), they may not want to trouble you, even if you are willing to baby-sit.

You know you're a grandma when ...

— you have fingerprints below your doorknobs.

— you volunteer to baby-sit.

— your daughter-in-law is still not good enough, but she looks better all the time.

— you ride a roller coaster for the first time in twenty-five years.

6

The Key:
Keep in Touch!

For, finally, we are as we love.
It is love that measures our stature.
— William Sloane Coffin, minister

Keeping in touch is the key to how active grandmas stay active. Following are some fun ways to do it, no matter where you live.

Make Plans for Every Holiday!

Celebrate together — not necessarily in person. Did you ever linger at the greeting card store and wander into strange and unusual categories? Now you know someone who will dearly love to receive a card with a jack-o'-lantern on it! Here is your chance to carve a pumpkin again, even if you live alone. Be sure to send a photograph of your creation so you can all enjoy it.

Be part of the fun at Easter by dyeing eggs with your grandchildren. If you can't be together, dye some eggs anyway and tell your grandchildren in an Easter card how you decorated them. Some gift stores celebrate the season by dressing someone up in a rabbit costume and offering free Polaroids with children. During Hanukkah, send them chocolate gelt and ask their parents to give them each a "coin" from you after lighting the candles each night. At Christmas, go to the mall and get your picture taken with Santa. Why not? Just tell Santa's helpers that you're a child at heart then send the photo to your grandchildren.

Start celebrating your birthday again. Have them count down with you. Make a birthday cake and tell them all about it. Ask them to make you a card by hand. This could even be an excuse for a visit. Remind your children that in Hawaiian families, all the relatives gather on Grandma's birthday for a party that lasts for days!

The holiday season is the busiest time of year for my mother's therapy practice. She says holiday stress can be lessened by remembering that it's the small family rituals that are the most important, not the yearly feat of pulling off the big meals and gatherings. Survive the holiday seasons by emphasizing the love over the "perfect" plans. Be flexible. And have fun!

It's funny how we go through phases of celebrating holidays.

When you are little, you count down to them with glee. Holidays are what separates the days from, well, all the other days. When you are dating, holidays are an excuse for social events. When you are married, they become a new ritual. Not long after that, you get busy and skip them altogether. Then you have children and start all over again. By the time you have grandchildren, you understand the importance of rituals. You know how to celebrate, too!

Call Them!

Call to say good morning or good night — without talking to the folks. Your grandchild will feel important to get a person-to-person phone call. Having someone who loves them at the other end of the line is an extra bonus. That will be one special phone call! Rest assured, the call can be short (meaning inexpensive). After all, you don't need to discuss world peace—and if you do, what better audience?

Even infants like to hear your voice. Don't be hurt if they're not in the mood to have the phone laid to their ear; tomorrow they might actually "talk" to you. There's no dictionary for babyspeak, so just assume they're saying "I love you."

My mother is convinced babies say "I love you" with their very first babble. Catherine, my one-year-old, sings what sounds convincingly like "I love you" nearly twenty-four hours a day. Yes, even on the telephone. I'm not sure she knows what she's saying, but I admit, I love it.

In any case, if you let your grandchildren know you love them, it won't be long until they really are saying "I love you."

Write Letters!

Whether you are down the block or across the country, all you need is a stamp to show you care. A letter can be many things, from a short note on a shopping list to a postcard of a frog. Once, my mother cut a heart from a blank deposit slip and mailed that. Juliette got the message.

Grandma Claire got the idea for mailing letters to her grandchildren when she was a little girl spending the summer away at camp in Maine. Her bunkmate's grandmother sent articles, pictures, and comics in the mail. My mother was jealous and decided to be that kind of grandma when she grew up. See? Grandmas have far-reaching influence. Maybe your grandchildren will pick up this fun habit and do the same for their grandchildren. And so on ...

Even if your grandchildren can't read yet, receiving mail will make them feel important. They will love being read a message that is especially for them. Once they memorize the contents (quicker than you might think), they will pretend to read it to themselves. Preschoolers will enjoy recognizing some letters of the alphabet and will be motivated to learn to read. For elementary-age children, not only will getting the letter be fun, but reading it will also be good practice.

If you'd like to write, but aren't sure what to say, mention times you shared recently or activities coming up. Writing is like courting — talk about them a lot and include yourself whenever you can!

Remember Their Friends

Write down the names of your grandchild's friends. Ask about the friends by name. Even if, as with many children, their friends change weekly, at least one name will probably remain consistent. Your grandchild will appreciate that you cared enough to try. Think how pleased you'd be if your grandchildren asked about your friends!

Learn Your Grandchild's Schedule

Remember on what day dance class falls. Then, when you call, write, or see them in person, you can ask about how their day went. If you ever have the opportunity, visit their class so you know what the experience is like.

My daughter is one of those children who will answer "fine" until the cows come home. Grandma Claire solves this dilemma by asking her about specific activities with one vital detail glaringly wrong. She'll ask what Juliette did at Casey's house when, in fact, she knows very well Juliette had been at Tara's home. Juliette will boil over with frustration and not only straighten Grandma out as to whose house she played at, but what activity they did there. Sometimes it's most clever to act like you're not so clever.

Emphasize Things in Common

I used to think my mother was crazy when suddenly, and for no apparent reason, she'd smile at Juliette and blurt out that both she and Juliette loved chocolate ice cream. For one thing, who doesn't like chocolate ice cream? For another thing, why tell me now? Finally, why tell me at all? At dinner, when Juliette wasn't hungry, Grandma would talk about how both she and Juliette hate spinach. At the pool, she'd point out that she had green in her bathing suit, and Juliette had green in her hat. While helping with bath time, Grandma would say she has soft skin on her shoulders just like Juliette, and then they would take turns feeling how soft they were. They were driving me nuts!

Finally it dawned on me. Every time my mother mentioned something — anything — that she and her granddaughter had in common, Juliette smiled. Whether it was that they both hate sand in their shoes, they both like bubble gum, or they both love getting mail, it made no difference. The more, the better. Juliette loves having things in common with her grandma. Now SHE points out things they have in common. Perhaps this game helps develop cognitive thinking. The important part is that it makes them feel close. The best part is that it's easy. Try it, you'll see.

Send Teeny-Tiny Mementos

Kids love getting surprises. Stickers, a headband, or colored shoelaces are tangible proof you care. My three-year-old insists presents are wrapped, surprises are not. Even a box of raisins can be a good surprise — almost anything unexpected is a treat.

However, if you are a frequent visitor, don't bring gifts every time. Your grandchildren should look forward to you, not the gift. After all, you are the best gift they'll ever have. If you have more spending money than the parents, help where it counts, with diapers or dancing class.

If you still can't resist, once in a while treat the parents to some unexpected goodies such as fresh bagels or real maple syrup. They need attention, too.

Share Your Favorite Childhood Book

Be forever connected to that favorite story in their minds. Don't let them keep it with their other books. It should have a special place to live so that it has a special place in their heart.

Teach Your Favorite Song

Kids are not music critics; they won't care what your voice sounds like. They will, however, remember your song and they'll feel close to you when they sing it, no matter where you are. If they happen to hear the song somewhere else, you can be sure they'll be thinking of you.

Get Personal with Gifts

Give gifts the children want — not just what you want them to have. Every year, Juliette receives a beautiful dress for her birthday from her great-grandma and great-grandpa. This year, they asked what else she liked and I mentioned her infatuation with Barney, the purple dinosaur. Her birthday turned into a Barney bonanza, and she was the happiest little girl in America. Generally shy with relatives she doesn't see often, Juliette couldn't wait to talk to Great-grandma and Great-grandpa on the phone. They took an active role in her life and she won't soon forget. Oh, they also sent a beautiful dress!

If your grandchild longs for something you or the parents disapprove of, ask for another suggestion. Just remember, the more personal you get, the more your grandchild will relate to you. Making a wish come true is a signal you know them well. In turn, your grandchildren will want to know you better.

Don't insist your grandchild share her gift right away. Would you share your new cashmere sweater before you wore it? The child may be too young to have progressed through the mine/yours/ours phases of early childhood. You can encourage them to share a few toys, but it's okay to have some special ones.

Give gifts with no strings attached. Don't expect anything in return. Feel free to ask about the gift when you speak with your grandchild. If they loved it, they may attach those emotions to you. But don't think of your gift as a bribe. Try not to be disappointed if they exchange it for something else or give it to their best friend. Your goal is to make them happy. They'll share their happiness with you!

You know you're a grandma when ...

— your idea of a good time includes microwave popcorn and a video of singing animals.

— you stop worrying about what people will think.

— your children no longer clean up before you visit.

— when shopping, your feet automatically take you to the children's department.

7

How to Really Help: the Children, the Parents, and You

Do and you shall be.

— **Camus**

Be and you shall do.

— **Sartre**

Do be do be do.

— **Frank Sinatra**

Your duties as a grandma are divided among your grandchildren, your children, and yourself. The most vital concern for all of you is safety. Classes in infant and child CPR and emergency first aid are available through your local Red Cross chapter as well as many hospitals and YMCAs. Libraries and video stores often rent tapes on child safety free as a public service. Once you have the safety foundation, you will be free to focus on the fun part — the relationships.

For the Grandchildren
Sense of Self

Have you ever been at a cocktail party where the woman next to you said, "Hi, nice party. So, what do you do?" Then, based on your answer, you watched the wheels turn in her head until something clicked and she decided whether you were worth talking to, or excused herself to put more dip on her cracker.

Now, pretend you are five years old. A girl with a shovel comes over to you at the park and says she'll play with you if you can build a sand castle. That's a lot of pressure, isn't it? You want to play, but you're not quite sure if you can build a sand castle. Are you capable? Will you ever be capable? Your identity and self-esteem are at stake. This pressure is enough to dissuade you from ever trying to build one.

Let the children know you value them for who they are, not what they are capable of doing. Be proud of your grandson's batting average or school grades. But love him no matter what. Next time you are at a party and someone asks what you do, reply that mostly you enjoy talking to people who don't ask you that question. Then walk away. Find a telephone, call your grandson, and tell him you love him — before he gets a chance to brag about his home run.

My mother has a sign in her home that reads: "I'm proud of what you've done but even more of what you are."

Unconditional Love

This should be listed as an FDA nutritional requirement for children. Telling them you'll love them more if they clean up their mess on your carpet is called Performance-based Affection. It is called The Reward System. It is also called Bribery. Do they have to bribe you for your love? Do you bribe them to love you with toys and treats? No, those things are extra. Your grandchildren love you for just being you.

Hear this! When a child seems the least lovable, that's the time when he needs your love most. Give him a hug. Be loving, in good times and bad. You can be a rock of emotional support in the stormy sea of childhood.

Comfort Zone

Hooray, being a grandma means no more endless battles with kids! Now the little ones can run from mean old Mommy to you. You can be the softy. Not exactly good cop/bad cop, but an all-around comfort zone — an escape from the day-to-day realities of discipline and growing up.

Whenever my mother hears babies crying, she wants to pick them up right away and comfort them. "Even at the market, I'm tempted to pick up strangers' babies when they cry and the parents don't respond. I used to be tough. Now I'm a cream puff." Of course, one of the advantages to being a grandma is that you don't have to listen to babies crying all the time.

As long as you are not interfering or undermining the parents' discipline, feel free to comfort your grandchildren.

Validation

You can give the Grandma Stamp of Approval to everything good your grandchild does. Everyday battles over putting toys away can evolve into proud accomplishments when you validate the behavior. Pleasing you is special. With you to brag to, those tough tasks will not seem so hard after all.

Even other children will seek your validation. For example, Grandma Sue attends every holiday party at her granddaughter's preschool. When she missed St. Patrick's Day, the other children missed her, asking, "Where's Grandma Sue?" It might be a party without you, but it won't be the same.

Tolerance

When you've seen it all before, it takes a lot to raise your eyebrows. Your grandson's imaginary dinosaur isn't so alarming when you think back to your daughter's invisible friend, which probably once concerned you the same way your grandson's behavior concerns your daughter now. Offer this tolerance to your grandson, and your daughter will be able to relax as well. Many disturbing trends crop up throughout the different stages of growing up. Your grandchild will benefit from your relaxed attitude. After all, if you don't make a big deal out of your grandchild's eccentricity, it most likely won't last long enough to be harmful.

Remember the old adage that the strictest parents were the wildest ones in their youth? Here is your chance to savor your child's comeuppance. As a grandma, you can just smile like the Cheshire cat, say nothing, and feel saintly. Tolerance is a learned behavior — and a gift for others, as well.

Time

Oh, where do the hours go? Your children are rushing between work, family, and (if they're lucky) friends. The phone, the fax, the groceries, the jobs ... the only thing that doesn't stop is the clock. No wonder divorce is so prevalent — the couple rarely has time for intimacy. Most parents dream of leisurely picnics in the park with the kids. Didn't you? Now is your chance. Being a grandma means you get to savor the time you have to hang out with your grandchildren. You can have real conversations about the cosmos and their place in it. The more you know them, the better you'll like them. Your grandchildren will appreciate your time and attention, and you all the more. Sounds clichéd, but then, where do clichés come from? The truth. Give the gift of time.

For Your Children

Emotional Support

Good parenting is a difficult task. Just as children need parents for support, the parents also need someone to turn to. Who can we call when the baby cries all night? Who can we confer with when it is time to discuss AIDS and birth control? On the other hand, who will rejoice with us when the baby sleeps through the night? Or when the teenager turns down a drink and tells you about it? Who will under-stand — and care? Encourage your children to turn to you, in good times and bad. They need you.

Authority

You have already experienced parenthood, so you are the best one to give advice. This does not mean your children must follow your advice. It does, however, empower them to cite your opinion to their children. Never contradict or insult the parents in front of your grand-children. The conflict will only confuse and hurt the little ones, who automatically believe what you say. After all, if you taught Mommy or Daddy everything they know, you must be a genius! Never abuse this authority.

Pressure Valve

When your children are on overload, you can be a lifesaver. When the laundry is piled high, bills are stacking up, and dinner is boiling over, you can pick up the fussy infant, offer a toy to the whiny toddler, and lovingly tease the sarcastic teenager. You can take them all outside for a bubble-blowing contest or a short hike. Their parents may need to deal with just one child for a few minutes. They may need to get dinner on the table. They may just need some time to relax. So, put on your sunblock and safety whistle. Grandma's here to save the day!

If you are far away, you can be just as much help as a sounding board. If possible, get an answering machine with a speaker phone built in. This way, whenever your daughter or your son needs to let off some heat, they can vent to you while you peruse your favorite magazine. Remember to say "my goodness" a lot!

Sometimes I'm too embarrassed to talk to a friend and too grumpy to unfairly harass my husband, so I'll call my mother. She'll either help put things in perspective or get me thinking about something completely different. For instance, once I've spilled my guts, it's wonderfully distracting to discuss my mother's next opportunity to have the kids all to herself. Sometimes Mom tells me about resorts she'd like to visit and we plan imaginary vacations. We even determine how warm it is, how the wind feels on our faces, and how soft the lounge chairs are. You don't need to be a professional to help your children; being a caring grandma is enough.

Negotiator
As the family matriarch (or the Supreme One, as we say), you naturally have everyone's best interests in mind. So, when a fierce battle is raging between your children and theirs, you are the ideal person to arbitrate. Even with conflicts over one-sided parental demands — such as choosing a bedtime story, completing chores, or going to bed — you can be a big help. If your youngest grandchild is screaming to stay up later, negotiate for a nap the next day. If she doesn't want naps at all, bargain for an earlier bedtime. With younger children, you can make a compromise feel like a victory.

If your relationship with your child's mate is good, you can help them, as well. Be fair, but don't go overboard. My mother is so fair, she often sides with my husband. When asked, you can help from behind the scenes by offering your child some positive ways to work out the situation.

My mother used to show a film to her family development students at Ohio State University. The film showed a couple resolving conflict in three ways: accommodation — giving in; compromise — each getting something less than they want; and taking turns (her favorite). One common characteristic of dysfunctional families is that they never resolve the argument, they just move on. Whether the conflict is between your child and your grandchild or your child and their spouse, invite them to state their feelings, then think of ways to solve the problem. Ask them what's more important, being right or having a relationship.

At my house, the biggest fights have to do with who's making dinner. In other words, I don't want to. Hey, we're living in the nineties! However, since we have children, somebody has to cook. My mother suggested writing down a schedule for which nights I had to cook and which nights I didn't. My husband agreed, content that he could count on some hot meals without the side dish of resentment. I cook about the same amount now, but I enjoy it more now that I know I don't have to. Schedules work for chores as well as such things as who's turn it is to pick out the rental video. Even if you don't always adhere to the schedule, you've cleared the air, and everyone realizes the value of cooperation.

Heroine

You are the best one to call in an emergency. You know where everything is ... and you care. Even if you can't be present physically, you can help the adrenaline-addled parent solve the problem with your wise suggestions.

When I demonstrated a cartwheel for my three-year-old and cut my foot on the hammock frame, life at our house turned upside down. For a week I was on crutches, unable to put an ounce of weight on my stitched-up foot. That translates into not being able to carry anything, from my nursing baby to a glass of water. After several days of juggling babysitters, camping out on my bed eating delivered pizza and whatever else my daughter could drag in from the kitchen, the weekend finally came. My husband fumigated the house, made breakfast, then fainted at the sight of the laundry pile. To give him a little credit, between me and the kids he did have his hands full . (After all, he isn't a mother!) Thank God for Grandma Claire. When her work week was over, she drove up with a homemade lasagna and did about eight loads of laundry. Then she went home for a golf date. My mother, my hero.

Sometimes you might feel torn about dropping everything to play heroine. That's okay. No one expects you to help every time; after all, you have your own life and personal obligations. And the young family should develop a network of support in case of emergency. The point here is that you do it best — and we appreciate you the most.

Friend

It's true: finally you can be friends. You may not want to share the intimate details of your sex life, but certainly you can chat about your favorite gown at the Academy Awards. When your focal length extends past your child to your grandchild, all that parental grief loosens up and, if you let it, dissolves into thin air — at least enough to start a new, improved relationship. Your child's emotional baggage, the myriad wrongs you supposedly committed, are no longer in the foreground. Be friends.

For You
Understanding the Grandchildren

How many times have you heard someone tell you their child's behavior is just a phase he or she is going through? Go ahead, roll your eyes. Most times, however, it is just a phase. The trick is to know which phase it is, what it means, and whether it should be encouraged or simply endured. After all, loving children — and adults — is easier when you understand them.

Here is a simplified version of the socioemotional developmental stages defined by renowned child development expert Erik Erikson. Each stage of development offers a critical period, a time when a certain skill must be achieved in order to lay the groundwork for future success.

Keep in mind that each child must learn at his or her own rate. The toddler who seems slow to toddle may be a large baby with extra weight to carry when walking. The child may be busy observing and thinking — in other words, learning. Children develop at different speeds, but in the same general progression.

Failure to accomplish the goals of each stage can have far-reaching effects well beyond childhood.

0 to 18 Months — Building Trust

The initial stage of life is existence, which obviously takes a lot of adjustment. It is amazing how quickly a baby advances during the first year. An infant's primary behavior is reaching, usually for the caregivers (bonding).

Goal: Emotional security.

Challenge: A baby is hungry and cries. The crying stops on seeing Mother or hearing her footsteps because the baby trusts her for food. Mistrust comes from prolonged discomfort and anxiety — waiting too long for needs to be met.

Grandma's Role: To love, nurture, and be consistent.

Appropriate Gifts: Soft, cuddly security blankets or dolls; textured and colorful items that help the child to explore the senses; large, soft balls to encourage eye-hand coordination.

18 Months to 3 Years — Building Autonomy

Becoming an individual means demonstrating power by doing "by myself": walking, climbing, grasping, and letting go. The child also learns to control bodily functions. Self-pride leads to strutting, talking, and enjoying jokes.

Goal: Feelings of self-worth lead to healthy curiosity and awe of life.

Challenge: If shamed by others, the child will doubt self, feel worthless, and give up curiosity about the world.

Grandma's Role: Praise the child. Offer choices to show you respect the child's opinion. Watch the child practice such new behavior as stacking objects.

Appropriate Gifts: Blocks, pegboards, and finger paints for developing motor skills; character figurines, trucks, and tea sets for imaginative play.

4 to 5 Years — Initiative

As children move from attachment to exploration, they question and seek experience with purpose. Dramatic play teaches about life. When children feel guilty, they often repeat their parents' voices, telling them what they may or may not do. By now they have developed a conscience. Too much control makes them fearful.

Goal: Curiosity leads to healthy exploration of the outside world, helping to create an understanding of the child's place within the world.

Challenge: If children are taught that the swimming pool is dangerous, they may develop a fear of water. If they are taught the safety rule of staying away from the pool unless a grownup is watching, then they will be free to explore water play when it is appropriate.

Grandma's Role: Talk with them, play with them, and encourage their small steps toward independence.

Appropriate Gifts: Learning toys: clay, puzzles, books, and dramatic play items, including dress-up, kitchen sets, train sets.

6 to Puberty — Industry

These children want to do things! They are learning what they are capable of: dressing themselves, completing schoolwork, painting, dancing, playing sports, etc.

Goal: Achievement builds confidence.

Challenge: Children who do not feel confident in their abilities, will soon feel inferior in all respects. This unworthiness will create a cycle of nonparticipation that eliminates further opportunity for achievement, leading to a sense of inferiority.

Grandma's Role: Applaud their accomplishments. Go to the park and to their ball games. When a child is unsuited to a particular skill, encourage participation in alternative activities where another opportunity for achievement exists.

Appropriate Gifts: Art and hobby kits plus other items tailored to individual interests.

Adolescence — Identity

Teenagers need to feel good about their sexually developing bodies. Feeling comfortable with themselves allows them to turn outward and care about things other than themselves. They struggle to find new values and beliefs, while rejecting those that don't quite fit. Healthy children learn to sympathize with other people. They develop genuine concern and commitment to the world around them.

> **Goal:** To love themselves and know what they stand for.
>
> **Challenge:** Teens with a poor sense of themselves search for belonging and can be led astray easily .
>
> **Grandma's Role:** Show consistent interest in them as they try on new identities despite the outrageous clothing and hairstyles this search might involve.
>
> **Appropriate Gifts:** Personalized items, trendy clothing, a session with a career counselor, a visit to a college of interest, leisurely walks ... time alone with you.

Young Adulthood — Intimacy

Love is the dramatic interest of this age group. Each of the previous stages have laid the groundwork: trust, autonomy, initiative, industry, and identity. Young adults can now be truly close to another human being in an intimate, committed relationship.

> **Goal:** The ability to be ethically and emotionally intimate with another.
>
> **Challenge:** Young adults need to allow themselves to be accepted and understood, or they risk remaining isolated all their lives.
>
> **Grandma's Role:** Be genuine and provide a shoulder to cry on. Be consistently loving and nonjudgmental as they struggle with major life decisions.
>
> **Appropriate Gifts:** Tickets for two for concerts, theater, or sports events; gift certificates for bookstores and music stores.

As you can see, your role is essentially the same throughout your grandchild's life: to love, nurture, and be consistent.

Adulthood — You

While babies develop, so do the rest of us. Parents, children, and grandparents go through different stages of the life cycle at the same time. Open yourself up to the exploration of you. Grandmas are just as important as their grandchildren. Recognizing where you are coming from and where you are going will help you lead the children in the right direction.

You know you're a grandma when ...

— you carry a larger purse just to fit all the photos.

— you start exercising again — so you can lift the baby.

— you buy Christmas or Hanukkah presents all year round.

— Your daughter answers the phone, "Hi, Mom."

— chicken pox don't make you nervous.

8

Simple Psychology

Children divine those who love them;
it is a gift of nature which we lose as we grow up.
— Paul de Kock,
L'Hommes aux trois Culottes

The Queen Mother

When your first child is expecting, you are the Queen. It's a delightful time for flitting about, rejoicing, bragging, and planning for the generation to come. Like all royalty, you bequeath your highest hopes on your future progeny.

The instant that baby is born, step aside! Smile while you do it, before someone gives you a shove whether you like it or not. Pass the baton graciously to the new Queen. You are now the Queen Mum!

Even though my mother taught child development for many years, she says, "I truly believe my daughter and son-in-law know the answers about their children's needs. Maybe that's because I was a Benjamin Spock mother. I met him once, and Dr. Spock agreed that parents know their babies better than anyone else." Read the literature, consult the experts, but remember, your children know their children best.

Wait! Your role is far from over: you are the sage, wise in the ways of parenting that remain mysterious for those newly installed on the throne. When you do have information you'd like to share:

— Wait for the right time.
— Ask if it's okay to make a suggestion.
— Use "I" statements. ("I would try it this way … ")
— Ask them to let you finish your whole thought.
— Finish by asking for their viewpoint.
— Assure them that the decision is theirs, and you'll support them regardless.

Projection

How do you feel when someone refers to you as a wonderful grand-mother? Anxious to hug and kiss your grandchildren, of course. What people expect of you often influences how you behave. This is called positive and negative projection.

Two types of negative projection affect children strongly: the first is called "limiting." If we refer to Juliette as the family artist and describe her little sister Catherine as the family athlete, what are the odds that Juliette will try out for the swim team or that Catherine will develop her drawing skills? Probably not so good. These kinds of comments and comparisons are difficult to avoid, but they can severely limit your grandchildren's growth. If we label children a certain way, we will treat them according to that label, both consciously and unconsciously. Worse yet, the children may hear us: any label used by such an authority figure as Grandma has a great impact. Ultimately, this selective treatment will hinder the children's success, which is based on both a child's self-image and other people's expectations. So, praise your grandchildren's talents, encourage their efforts, and leave it at that.

Part of your role as a grandmother is to encourage your grand-children to define themselves. Encourage them to explore all kinds of activities. Have them tell you their feelings about who they are and what they like by asking them questions and listening to their answers. When my mother asked Juliette if she'd like to be a doctor, like her mother's friend, Juliette said no. Instead of regaling the joys of medicine, Mom simply asked, "Why not?" Juliette explained she didn't want to give shots. It was a valid point. It ended any push for medicine and opened the larger issue: what does she want to be when she grows up?

The other kind of negative projection is defining. The nursery rhyme "sticks and stones may break my bones, but words can never hurt me" is entirely untrue. In fact, negative words can *define* a child, especially when it comes from an authority like Grandma.

When Joey is accused of being a bad boy for hitting his friend, will he realize that it was only the act of hitting that was bad? Probably not. The real danger is that Joey may believe he is bad and live up to the title, creating a self-fulfilling prophecy. Always respond to a child's unwanted behavior by addressing the action, not the child. Words like stupid and idiot — even in jest — will stick, especially from you. The child may wrap his whole identity around that word. Say something nice, even when you're angry. "That was a bad thing to do, kiddo." Or "honey", "cutie", "jellybean" — something. Anything!

The late Dr. Haim Ginott, a child development expert, constantly reminded adults to let the child know, "I love you, but I don't like your behavior." By phrasing your criticism in those terms, you are validating a child's self-worth instead of insulting him. You tell the child that he is more valuable than the behavior itself, and you want to help him modify his behavior so he'll have happier relationships with others.

If your granddaughter spilled her milk, don't say she's clumsy. Let her know you don't enjoy cleaning it up and ask her to help you. Tell her you love her but you don't love wiping up milk. If she did it on purpose, consider a time out. Ask her to be more careful next time and wait for her to agree.

The real issue at stake is self-esteem — *always* build it up. Don't let your grandson see you wince at his new haircut. Remark at the fact that he got a haircut and ask if it was fun. Sidestep your negative opinion. If he corners you by asking how you like the haircut, tell him you think he's beautiful, inside and out.

Positive projection has a tremendous influence on children. Good girl, smart girl, pretty girl, responsible girl — these kinds of compliments will enhance your granddaughter's self-image and help her to grow up good, smart, confident, and responsible. Image boosting is equally important for children of both sexes.

A recent survey of women who are successful public figures and politicians revealed the same conclusion. These women grew up hearing how special they were. They were told, almost to the one, that they could accomplish anything they put their minds to. The survey result serves as another illustration of how positive projection works.

My mother's private practice draws individuals of all types involved in many different situations. Her use of psychotherapy examines one's background by exploring the individual's experiences within the family system. When she asks her clients, men and women, "Who believed in you?" the common answer is, "My grandmother."

Reflexive Listening

This is easier than it sounds: when your three-year-old mermaid proudly exclaims, "I swimmed across the pool the whole way!" repeat her sentence back with enthusiasm. Say, "You swam across the pool the whole way! That's wonderful!" The technique works with nearly any comment in any conversation. The child will be sure that you understand and really did hear her. This type of response validates both of you. As an extra bonus, she'll hear the corrected version of her sentence without being chided. After all, if she thinks she'll get an English lesson whenever she talks to you, most likely she'll stop talking.

This practice starts in infancy when a child points to a door, says "door," and you repeat the word back to her. You may be surprised at the number of situations in which reflexive listening comes in handy — and not just with your grandchildren!

Consistency

Beware! Everyday we ask people how they are without really caring. Many times we don't even wait for an answer. So, if you tell your grandchildren you've missed them, then ignore them, they'll naturally assume you didn't miss them at all. But they won't chalk it up to good manners — they'll think you are a liar. And the truth is they'll be right. If you didn't miss them (maybe you just saw them yesterday), don't tell them you did. It's best to let your behavior be consistent with your words.

Grandma Sara refers to her grandchildren as "jewels" in her crown. This description makes Becky, one of Sara's grandchildren, feel both honored and loved. Around friends, Grandma Sara does treat Becky as a treasure — and Becky loves to dress up and be paraded around at Grandma Sara's country club. Unfortunately, Grandma Sara doesn't pay much attention to Becky any other time. You might say Becky is getting a mixed message: maybe Grandma Sara really doesn't love her after all. Possibly Sara just doesn't know how to relate to children. But whatever the reason, take note! Treat your grandchildren the same whether you are alone with them or in public. Don't confuse them with mixed messages and always be aware of their feelings. They are more than mere jewels in your crown.

Praise

You might brag about your grandchildren to others, yet fear complimenting them directly. Perhaps you've heard that praise brings bad luck or spoils the child. Actually, the reverse is true: praise is invaluable.

Grandchildren are the dividends of motherhood. You invested a lot of love and perspiration in raising your children, and your little heirs are a fair reward. Love can't spoil them. So, reinvest your love with your grandchildren to help you all reap even greater dividends down the road.

Every Child Is Special

Each child deserves individual attention. Let her know she is special all by herself. Emphasize what makes her so special — the color of her eyes, her double-jointed thumb, even the way she loves to watch birds. When you ask a child to wait until her brother is finished speaking or playing with you, remind her she is just as special as he is and you want to give her every bit of your attention when it's her turn.

Feeling special builds security. Every child needs to feel safe within herself so she can move on to trust the world around her. Only by truly understanding how special she is can she learn as an independent self.

Do you remember the joy on your child's face when she took her first steps? That is the joy of competency — the feeling of satisfaction from a job well done. Once a child feels emotionally secure, she can begin her journey toward autonomy. You can share the joy of your grandchild's first steps in the real world. Not only are you proud of her accomplishments, you are also partly responsible for her success. By making her feel special, you enable her to conquer the world. That makes you pretty special, too.

Sibling Rivalry
New Baby

Do not — I repeat, not — rush to the new baby! Restrain yourself. The baby will not remember this, but big brother will. He might very well punish you for behaving so badly. He might ignore you or withhold his affection. You'll have to be patient to win him back, and it won't be easy. Instead, love up Number One. Emphasize what a wonderful big brother your grandson is, and how lucky his baby sister is to have him. Hug him, kiss him, give him a special "I'm a big brother" T-shirt. Then go ahead and coo over the baby all you want!

Competition

Don't let siblings vie for your attention. Let them know you have unlimited interest in each one of them, and taking turns lets you concentrate especially on them. Be careful when you give presents. For older children, make sure that your gifts complement their individual interests. That way each child knows you are paying attention and you care specifically about him or her. With younger children, similar or matching gifts are best to prevent any comparisons to discover whom you like best. Competition can be healthy — but not when it comes to love.

Playing Favorites

When I was nine months pregnant with my second child, I went to a birthday party for my friend's son Cody. Four generations were represented at the party, and I had the opportunity to sit and chat with both the grandmother and the great-grandmother. I told them I was nervous that I wouldn't have the same incredible amount of love for the new baby as I had for the first. The women assured me I would.

"What happens when you have more than one grandchild?" I asked.

"You automatically favor the first grandchild," replied the grandma.

"Hmmm," I thought.

As we watched the children play, the great-grandma spoke up. "That's not true. You love them all equally." She turned to her daughter-in-law. "You're just a beginner. You'll see."

Grandma Claire holds her first granddaughter dear, but relates to her second because she herself is also a second child. Each child is special in his or her own way, for many different reasons.

Connecting Creatively

You can enjoy an imaginative relationship with your grandchild in many ways. One way is to allow them the freedom to make choices about things when no one correct answer exists. For instance, you can let them choose what to have for lunch. With younger children, simplify their decision making by limiting their options. Feel free to suggest such funny food combinations as a peanut butter-spaghetti sauce sandwich. With older children, let them make the most out of this freedom by helping you make that peanut butter-spaghetti sauce sandwich. If the sandwich is truly ghastly, they won't eat it. If it's actually edible, they can catch up on their nutrition plan later. Either way they'll love you for indulging their imaginations.

Another way to use creativity in your relationship is to play make-believe games. Salvage those old clothes you can't part with, and maybe some of those you can't wait to part with. Keep them in a trunk for the children's visits or send them off to their house. Not only will dress-up be fun, but it will remind them of you every time they play. Now, you might be thinking, "I'm not so self-centered that the children have to always be thinking of me." The truth is, thinking about you is healthy for them. As their grandma, you represent security, roots, and a positive connection to something larger than themselves. Maybe they'll make believe they are you!

Going with the Flow

My mother maintains if you've planned something for the children's fun, yet they're enjoying something else on the way, why make them stop? If they're having a wonderful time picking up every twig and leaf on their slow-motion walk, why make them hurry up to have fun someplace else? If lunch at Red Robin turns out to be a hit, does missing the Children's Museum matter? If the only one who cares is you, let it go.

When Juliette was four, Mom took her to see the Nutcracker ballet. This outing was a special event that took planning as well as tickets. After twenty minutes, Juliette needed to visit the bathroom and saw a television monitor of the show in the lobby. Grandma Claire was disappointed, but she also realized Juliette was perhaps too young for the occasion. Juliette sat in Grandma Claire's lap in the lobby and watched the ballet on television for a few minutes before they left. They created a warm and unexpected memory together that they talk about often. That's the important thing.

Going with the flow also applies to toys. Just because the manufacturer had something specific in mind doesn't mean your grandchild should. As long as the toy has some sort of play value and the child is enjoying it, applaud the creative approach. Who says the colored rings must fit over the post? For now, maybe your grandchild has more fun teething on them, lining them up in a row, or throwing them like Frisbees. Feel free to demonstrate how nicely they do stack on the post, in case it's not apparent, but let the child take over from there. Go with the flow.

You know you're a grandma when ...

— your sun visor doubles as a magic safety hat.

— the owner of the educational toy store sets things aside for you.

— you look forward to waking up early with your grandchildren.

— you buy Cheerios in bulk.

— your children count on you to help clean up before you leave.

9

Grandma Fun

No cowboy was ever faster on the draw than a grandparent
pulling a baby picture out of a wallet.
— Anonymous

It's fun to be a grandmother, because nothing is legally required of you. The opportunities listed below are yours to take advantage of as you like. Remember, the more you give of yourself, the more you'll be invited to share in the joys children offer.

Official Biographer

When the children cry, "Tell me a story!" what comes to mind? "Jack and Jill," "The Three Little Pigs," "Cinderella?" How about real stories guaranteed to make their eyes grow wide and your heart beat pitter-pat? Stories about your children will entertain them more than make-believe, and these stories will help your grandchildren see their folks in a gentler light.

Tell them about your daughter's first visit from the Tooth Fairy, when she cried because she wanted her tooth back. Tell them about your son's third birthday party, when he smeared cake all over his face. Stories like these will trigger warm memories for you — things you may have forgotten. You'll enjoy your children all over again. You'll remember the pains you went through to cheer up your daughter and how much trouble it was to make your son's clown-shaped cake. You'll feel pride at the considerate things you did and realize that, despite your natural misgivings, you really were a good parent.

You also have the opportunity to set the record straight. For years, I've pointed at our neighbor's Irish setter and told my daughter I had one when I was little. It was my mother who corrected my dwarfed view of history. The truth be told, Willie Wagtail was a cocker spaniel. I was so little, I assumed the dog was huge. As with many other elements of history, I have to believe my mother. After all, she was there.

Wizard

Anything can be magical — you're the wizard, so you can decide. Can you make a perfect piece of cinnamon toast? Call it magic. Is there a silly dance step the women in your aerobics class perform? Call it a magic step and teach it to your grandchild. Is there an old scarf you don't wear but can't bear to part with? Call it your magic scarf and let your grandchild wear it. It will help dry up tears from scraped knees and make any day special.

I'll never forget the sparkling rubies hidden in the sand at my nursery school in Tucson. The school's director was my surrogate grandma, and she told marvelous tales about those "rubies." They were buried treasure, left by pirates. I can't remember the details, but I'll never forget the crystals, or that wonderful woman. Even though I know they might have just been some spilled beads, I wish I would have saved some. Because of that woman, that playground was magical, and I think of it every time Juliette plays in the sand.

Grandma Claire always finds things in Juliette's ears. Big Bird lives there sometimes, and other times it's Minnie Mouse. Poor Juliette can never see for herself, but she trusts Grandma's words. Maybe you can do real tricks, like picking coins or candy out of your grandchildren's ears. Whatever the case, use your imagination, and your grandchild will, too.

What, You Again?

One of the privileges of being a grandma is that you can call your children as often as you like ... as long as you ask for your grandchildren. I admit, sometimes I get jealous and demand my turn. Doesn't my mother want to know how my day went? Meanwhile, when your grandchild sees Mommy stop everything to answer the phone — yet the call is for her — she will be thrilled.

Sometimes children don't want to talk. On those days, just send a message that you love them, hang up, and call back another time. Don't pressure them, or they'll resent it and never want to speak with you on the phone. One day, when Juliette had already spoken with Grandma and the telephone rang once again, I handed the phone to Juliette and told her it was Grandma Claire. Juliette shook her head and asked, "What, you again?" We're still laughing. Now it's one of Grandma's favorite stories. And believe me, she has a few.

Spitting Image

You call the shots in the looks department. Who does your grandchild really look like? Those aren't Daddy's ears, are they? No, they really came from your brother, the fireman. The brains, of course, came from you. Kids love to hear this stuff. It makes them proud. It gives them a sense of being part of a bigger picture. The mere shape of their chin connects them to other important people. Where did that dimple come from, anyway? I'll bet you know!

Sex Appeal

There are two popular images of grandmothers: the old-fashioned one shows a dumpy grandma with her hair in a silver bun, surrounded by screaming children; a modern one shows a sexy gal holding a tennis racquet, with no time for kids. Most grandmas are somewhere in between. One privilege of being a grandma is you can be as sexy as you want and still enjoy your grandchildren. Now you earn added respect because you're a grandma and you still look great.

You don't have to dress conservatively to be a "proper" mother anymore. Social taboos are behind you, whether you paid attention or not. Motherhood is proof of sexuality, after all. Sex is not a dirty word. It's the word that got us all here. Enjoy.

Shop 'til You Drop

Finally an excuse to shop anywhere, any time, for anything! Whether you're at Saks Fifth Avenue, KMart, or the corner grocery store makes no difference. Your grandchildren are always going to need bigger clothes, party shoes, a funny T-shirt, a new kite, a pop-up book, a cute greeting card, a fresh pack of gum ... the list is endless.

When your daughter admired your earrings, did you give them to her? If you are that kind of mother, this generosity can create trouble with your grandchildren. A word of warning here: Beware the slip of the tongue. Last week, Juliette admired my mother's yellow shoes. Automatically, she offered to buy her some to match. Now, she has to follow through. Spending the extra money is one thing. Finding canary yellow shoes in toddler size 10 1/2 is another. Juliette would have been perfectly happy with a "matching" canary yellow T-shirt or crayon. Grandma Claire says, "Next time, I'll just give her a kiss and say thank you."

Now is not the time to break the bank — next week the folks might hit you up for a new bicycle. Nevertheless, if you've got a dime, a stick of licorice with your grandchild's name on it is just waiting for you!

You know you're a grandma when ...

— you decide you can do without the new handbag — your granddaughter absolutely must have that darling pinafore.

— your arms feel empty, and you know its time for a visit.

— you feel beautiful, crow's-feet and all.

— you know the names of Pocahontas' sidekicks.

10

Your New Identity

A grandma is old on the outside and young on the inside.
— **John Wright, age seven and a half**

Who Are You, Really?

You're at the bank on a Friday afternoon. You look up and catch the eye of the young teller at window 4. He smiles. You smile back and try to concentrate on the scintillating bank services brochure. Then you wonder: what exactly did he see when he looked at you? Do you look like a grandma? At window 4, you identify yourself with your name, rank, and serial number: Judith Littleton, bank customer, account 777777. You're feeling friendly, but he seems tired and who are you to him, anyway? More importantly, who are you to you?

When you look in the mirror, who do you see? Forget the physical factors — they're transient. Who is behind those intelligent eyes?

Make a list of words that describe you. It might look like this:

corporate CEO
wife
feminist
friend
lover
intellectual
athlete
movie buff
bowling pro
shower opera singer
seamstress
championship shopper
gourmet chef
sister
mother
grandmother

Now, put those words in order of importance. The order may change from day to day. The significant ones won't. Examine your list.

These days, when many people start their own families in their thirties, motherhood lasts a pretty long time. So, you're likely to see yourself as a mother first and foremost. Your business role is important and has ego prominence, yet motherhood comes from the heart. But, like Hollywood says about classic films, you have transcended the genre. You've done motherhood one better. You are a grandma. Put it at the top of your list!

"Grandma" Means Power

Vanity Fair magazine introduced a former mayor in President Clinton's administration as a "grandmother of three." The game show *Wheel of Fortune* described a business owner as a grandmother before listing her professional credentials. Defining these accomplished women as grandmothers is not meant to demean them by bringing them down to a stereotypical female role; on the contrary, this identity gives them status in society. As a grandparent, you have roots in the past and influence on the future. You have power!

If you were to mention to the bank teller at window 4 that you are a brain surgeon, the young man will be impressed. He might be envious of your bank balance. He might wonder how you deal with all that blood. On the other hand, if you introduce yourself as a grandmother, he will hold you in esteem and think of his own grandmother. He will assume you are wise, capable of great love, and that you care about the world. If he knows you are a grandmother, you will get better service!

Mirror, Mirror

Relax, the pressure's off. How you look doesn't matter so much anymore. In fact, kids of a friend of mine were embarrassed to bring their grandma to Grandparents' Day at school because she didn't look like a "real" grandma — she was too young and pretty! At any rate, *please yourself.* You no longer have to compete with women whom gravity has never touched. Everyone's underarms will sag at some point. After all, you are a grandma now — your toned thighs are not what attracts adoration. You are!

If you are young and beautiful, don't fret over the title — especially with the grandchildren. If they hear you say you are too young to be a grandmother, they will figure you don't like them. After all, they know you are a grandma. If you like them, how could you be too young? Besides, being a young grandma is fun. You have the energy to keep up!

Grandma Claire didn't truly start an exercise regimen until after Juliette was born. She wanted to strengthen her arms to carry the baby more. She met other grandmas doing the same thing. "Now I want to stay in shape to make my girls proud," she explained. "Mostly, I want to stay healthy so I can enjoy a long, happy life with my grandchildren."

Free At Last

How many times have you heard the word eccentric paired with grandmother? Doing whatever you darned please is a natural outgrowth of living long enough and gaining self-confidence. With this identity comes liberation. No longer must you endure your children's harsh scrutiny. No longer do you have to dress respectably for the PTA. As a grandma, your job is to be fun and to have fun! Grandchildren don't embarrass easily. Now is your chance to greet the mailman in your bathrobe. Now is your chance to wear that silver-studded purple denim skirt, if that's your taste. Heck, Elizabeth Taylor does it! Now is your chance to try skydiving. Didn't Clare Luce Booth scuba dive during her eighties? Now is the time to please yourself. Let your children shake their heads and sigh, if they must. They are past being disgraced by you — now they can be amused. Like the song says — don't worry, be happy!

Qualifications

Your grandma status is proof you've made it through the rough parts of life. You've raised your family and worked hard for many years. You have vast experience and a genuine stake in the world. You have fulfilled your genetic imperative by producing future generations. Hold your head high. You're a Grandma!

You know you're a grandma when ...

— you stop worrying about grey hair.

— your grandson has a tantrum and you insist that it simply shows his independent spirit.

— you go on vacation with the grandchildren even if it means putting up with their parents all week.

— you trade your floral stationery for postcards with animals.

11

The Grandma Poll

Only a mother knows a mother's fondness.
— Lady Montague, 1754

A questionnaire was offered randomly to a group of religiously diverse families that ranged from lower to upper middle class. The survey addressed questions to both parents and grandmothers.

The parents were scattered around the country, with a majority residing in California. Most of these parents were not raised on the west coast: the grandmothers lived in Florida, New Jersey, Ohio, and states in between. Some had moved to be closer to the grandchildren.

The mothers tended to be in their late twenties or thirties, with children ranging in ages from one month to ten years. The number of grandchildren per grandmother ranged from one to ten, with the majority falling at four.

The most consistent response came not from the questions on the poll, but rather from the poll itself: the grandmothers were unanimously eager to talk about their grandchildren, while the parents felt the poll was a good excuse to speak with their folks. All things are not equal, however, and ninty-five percent of those responding to the poll were mothers.

Following are some of the questions from the survey and the answers they elicited.

1. Mom's mother is ... ___ nearby ___ far away
   Dad's mother is ... ___ nearby ___ far away
Sixty-five percent of maternal grandmothers lived nearby. Ten percent of paternal grandmothers lived nearby. Coincidence?

2. She is ... ___a lot of help ___ a nuisance ___ other
Maternal grandmothers were helpful; paternal grandmothers were generally "other" — not around much, but helpful when they were. These answers lent credence to the results of the question regarding proximity. However, they bring up a chicken-or-egg dilemma: are the maternal grandmothers helpful because they are close, or are they close because they are helpful?

3. Your favorite thing about Grandma is:

Maternal grandmothers were lauded for their emotional involvement: the love and adoration of the children. Parents were also grateful for having someone they could count on near by. Praise for paternal grandmothers more reflected the qualifications of the women themselves: they were "bright" with "common sense," they "knew the place," they were willing to help with almost anything, especially weaning babies to the bottle (the grandmothers preferred the bottle). Several were praised for being the stereotypical grandma who sewed, made dolls and quilts, and baked with the children. The most personal praise was for women who were thoughtful and supportive of the mother's maternal desires.

4. Your least favorite thing about Grandma is:

The number one complaint about grandmothers was that they live too far away. After that, the answers were evenly split between those mothers who received too much criticism and unwanted advice, and those who wanted more "insight based on past experiences" and more understanding and "knowledge about what kids do at various developmental stages." Other responses mentioned small town narrow-mindedness, wishy-washiness, and an "aversion to changing diapers."

5. Since you had kids, has your relationship with Grandma changed? How?

All mothers felt that their relationship with their own mother had improved since the grandchildren were born. Most felt they had finally earned respect as an adult. They also had more in common. Some felt it was better because the focus was no longer on them — it was now on the grandchildren. The mother's relationship with their mother-in-laws, for the most part, did not change, although some felt things were better. The greatest change was that, good or bad, grandchildren forced them to interact more.

6. What suggestions would you give to Grandma if you could?

Mothers were all over the map with suggestions for the grandmothers. More than a few requested unconditional love. Many wanted grandma to recognize that "kids are smart, so treat them that way." Many requested for an end to unwanted advice — including "recipes for homemade baby food." More than a few wanted to reassure grandma that their granddaughter was not fat — she was only six months old! A group of mothers were nervous about the length of time between motherhood and grandmotherhood and, to feel more comfortable having grandma baby-sit, wished she would learn infant

CPR and review emergency procedures.

Suggestions for paternal grandmothers were far more consistent. The first word in sixty percent of the responses was "relax." Mothers went on to reassure grandmas that kids "love you and remember you even though they don't see you much." Many included reminders that a baby's crying is no reflection on grandma. Others asked grandma to concentrate on enjoying the children rather than giving their folks grief.

Finally, it was grandma's turn ...

1. What's the best part of being a grandma?

27% The joy of loving the children.

27% Watching the children grow and develop their own personalities.

18% All the fun without all the responsibility — "when the baby starts crying you can go home."

9% Being loved by them — "getting return smiles that melt my heart."

9% Interacting with the children.

9% The extended family — "full and joyful holidays."

2. What's the worst part of being a grandma?

Eighty-one percent of respondents were emphatic that living far away or not seeing the grandchildren often enough was the worst part. The other nineteen percent felt there was nothing bad about being a grandparent.

3. Do you visit ... ___ anytime ___ call first ___ plan ahead?

Eighty-one percent planned ahead for visits, most likely because they lived far away. Ten percent called first, and nine percent visited anytime.

4. What are your favorite activities to do with your grandchildren?

36% Talking — interacting, making them laugh.

36% Taking walks, preferably one child at a time (which provides the opportunity to talk).

20% Cuddling and hugging.

8% An assortment of activities including playing on the floor, swimming, biking, teaching new things, going to the playground, and going on vacation to enjoy all these things.

5. What do you do differently now that you're a grandma?

The following answers were equally popular:

1. Knit.
2. Baby-sit.
3. Buy more presents.
4. Watch them instead of trying to get anything done.
5. Make plans with them in mind.
6. Think of them constantly — "they're number one in my life."
7. "Identify more with my daughter."
8. Think more of the future.
9. Shop for baby food.

6. What advice would you give to a new grandma?

The same two answers popped up over and over:

1. Relax and enjoy every minute of it — "it's the most fabulous thing in the world."
2. Don't interfere: "Don't try to be a mother again." "Cool it."

Other answers included reminders to not forget about sons and daughters — they need love and attention, too.

8. What surprised you most about being a grandma?

Twenty-seven percent were most surprised at their intense feelings of love for their grandchildren.

Other answers were about equal, including:

1. Everything.
2. Nothing.
3. The fact that they didn't have to be "old with grey hair in a bun" to be a grandma.
4. Difference in stamina.
5. All the grandchildren were "beautiful and outstanding."
6. "How wonderful it is."
7. Didn't think they were ready until it happened.

9. Has your relationship changed with your daughter-in-law/son-in-law?

60%   Said yes: they now had more understanding and respect for their daughter-in-law's opinions, and more confidence and admiration for their son-in-law's fatherly pride. Recognizing characteristics of the parents in the children makes the relationship easier for the grandparents.

40%   Said no: this answer emerged from the extremes of either having a great relationship already or not having much of a relationship at all.

10. What's the funniest thing that's happened to you as a grandma?

Most of the answers described the kind of situations where "you had to be there" to appreciate them. There were "pearls of wisdom" from three-year-olds, funny nicknames, brute honesty about nose hair, and a grandchild's request to inherit the backyard when the grandparents "expire." Many grandmas were amazed at how everything about birthing and childcare has changed since they were mothers.

Conclusion

This poll was by no means scientific; nevertheless, the results were consistent and reliable in terms of the average grandmother.

The most interesting result is the coincidence between the mothers' suggestions for grandmothers versus the grandmothers' suggestions for other grandmothers. The mothers asked the grandmothers to relax and enjoy the children and to stop interfering with unwanted advice. The grandmothers, without knowing about the preceding answers, suggested the very same things to other grandmothers.

This coincidence indicates one of two things: either grandmothers are not listening to themselves, or they are consciously trying to stop interfering. In some cases, grandmothers allowed that not interfering is "difficult." Indeed, you need a delicate balance to walk the fine line of offering advice. If you help too much, you can be interfering. If you don't help, you aren't interfering, but you aren't helping, either. Damned if you do, damned if you don't. You might as well err on the side of the children and help as much as you like.

The poll's most conclusive result is that everyone agrees grandmas aren't around enough. Take heed.

You know you're a grandma when ...

— you buy a new camera.

— you start baking again.

— Father's Day is at the kids' house.

— your clothes are perfect for "dress-up."

12

Long-Distance Grandmas

No one . . . who has not known that inestimable privilege
can possibly realize what good fortune it is
to grow up in a home where there are grandparents.
— Suzanne Lafollette, writer (1893 - 1983)

The biggest complaint about grandmas is that they live too far away!
The only advantage of being far away is that you might not worry so
much about the children: you know everyone has to solve their own
problems. However, if one of those problems is that you're too far
away, here are some things to keep in mind.

Common Concerns

Invitations. Don't wait for an invitation! You may have a long wait—and not because they don't want to have you, but because there is rarely a perfect time for a visit. Ask your daughter or son — and especially their spouse — when would be a good time for a visit. Give them some concrete dates to choose from. That way, you all make a commitment and the visit will happen.

The "Big Event." My mother's friend Louise is always talking about her grandchildren. She lives in Ohio; they live in Montana. She can't wait to see them, but they're not exactly right around the corner. Whenever they speak on the phone, her children always invite her to visit, but she isn't sure if they are sincere or just being polite. Since she isn't used to visiting them, she feels like she would be intruding to force herself on them without a good excuse. So she is waiting for a big event, such as graduation. Personally, I think she's holding out until a talk show host takes pity on her and reunites the family on network television!

Don't wait. The occasion doesn't have to be Christmas or Hanukkah or a family reunion. If families saw each other more often, reunions wouldn't be such a big deal, anyway. If you visit during an ordinary part of the year, you'll learn the routine. You'll become familiar with where the dentist, the dance class, and the grocery store are — you may even get to know some neighbors. On the next visit, things will feel much cozier for everyone and you can be more relaxed, as well as more helpful. Don't wait for a big event. You *are* the big event.

Bad blood. If strained relations are keeping you from seeing the grandchildren, rise above the situation. You love those children despite their parents' bad graces—the two are not related. Why should the children miss out? Don't let pride get in the way of those sweet kisses. You don't have to make up — some issues may never be resolved. Simply put the conflict behind you. If a disagreement is keeping you from your grandchildren, then you are losing. Love is waiting in your grandchildren's hearts with your name on it. It's yours, you deserve it — go get it!

Continuity. Remember how back in grade school a week seemed like a million years? Imagine what six months must feel like. See your grandchildren as often as you can. Strangers at the grocery store are constantly telling me to enjoy the children while they are babies, because those years go by so quickly. I smile, nod, thank them, then shake my head and head for the diaper aisle. I notice the time passing only when I develop a roll of film that was lost in my purse for a few weeks. The changes are startling.

You want to know the children, not just remember them as babies. You don't want to be remembered by what you gave them for their birthday. Photographs are wonderful, but your scrapbook will be a lot more fun if the pictures of your grandchildren include you.

The Visit

How long is too long? If the travel time is great, you are likely to stay awhile. If you are sleeping on the couch, one week is plenty. If your children have a guest room or you are staying elsewhere, go for two weeks—a longer visit would most likely be too much. Even if you are on great terms with everybody, having a house guest is not only a lot of work, but also very stressful. (Even good things can produce stress.) The stress level doubles when the guest is somebody's mother.

Make a plan. Letting your family know, in advance, the date you will be leaving will frame the visit as a controlled event. When you arrive, sit down with everyone to discuss your plans. (Do the same thing when they visit you.) Build some structure into the visit by defining the things that you really want to do. Without structure there is chaos. On the other hand, too much structure is no fun. Your daughter or son may have tickets for you to visit Hearst Castle or see the new play. Perhaps they have reserved a rental car for you. Commit to what you would like to do with or without them.

Be assertive about the type of visit you prefer. Do you want to relax as if on a real vacation, or do you want to get involved and be helpful? If you do want to help, let them know how. Explain that you don't feel safe driving with the children, so you won't want to drive car pools. But say that you would enjoy making dinner Wednesday night and taking everyone to brunch on Sunday. Or whatever you prefer. Maybe you'd like to help by getting the adults a glass of wine before dinner. Maybe you would enjoy giving the baby her bath or shopping with the ten-year-old for new shoes. Allow for choices.

My friend Lydia complained that her mother-in-law did the dishes Sunday night. I couldn't understand why this was a problem. Lydia explained to me she does the dishes every night, while her husband is only responsible for Sunday. Her mother-in-law wasn't helping her at all, she was just letting her son get out of his share of the work. So, be careful not to step on toes, even when you are helping. Be supportive of the one who's doing all the work.

Pace yourself. My mother goes gangbusters when we are together. She is fully capable of doing every activity with the kids for forty-eight hours. Then she can't move for three days. Remember, kids are accepting. They'll be just as happy lying on the couch with you, reading or watching cartoons, as long as you are together.

Real life. Let the children keep to their routines. Experience your grandchildren's life with them. Accompany them to their activities, unless your presence is embarrassing for them. No offense personally, but teenagers will appreciate it if you let them decide where you take them. Bowling might be off limits; gymnastics might be fun. On your turf, and as an adult, you automatically make this choice. Treat them with the same respect. You are on their turf.

Be Yourself. No matter who is visiting whom, don't try too hard to impress them. You want to get to know your real grandchildren; let them get to know the real you!

Extenuating Circumstances

If you cannot visit them and they cannot visit you, all is not lost. Plenty of people in nursing homes or without funds to travel cross-country enjoy good relationships with their grandchildren. How? By taking advantage of other means of communication.

Telephone Time. People tend to be more intimate on the telephone than in person. There are no eyes to judge you and no distractions. Call your long-distance phone company to find a frequent calling plan that will include your grandchildren's area. Or set up a regular Sunday evening phone date.

Teenagers love to talk on the telephone — especially if you talk about them. Ask about their boyfriends and their favorite new clothing style. Ask their opinions on movies and gun control and the President's latest veto. They'll appreciate someone who cares what about they think. Eventually, they are bound to get curious and ask about you.

Children love to talk on the telephone, too. Inquire about their friends and hobbies and what they had for dinner. Volunteer information about your day. Make up funny food combinations that you had for dinner, like octopus and cotton candy, and they'll go wild. Tell them stories about how you rode on a giant singing caterpillar with red fur and purple polka dots. If you're worried about how impressionable they are and fear you might be contributing to potential nightmares, confess that you're just being silly. They'll love you for it.

Pen Pals. Write letters that include stamped postcards for your grandchildren to send back to you. With any luck, they'll jot down a few words before they mail them. Younger children will feel important when they get your mail, and they will enjoy writing important letters back. Older children might not show it, but they'll enjoy the attention, too. Use Elvis stamps or something else fun and significant. If you ask your grandchild for specific information, such as what times they got in the swim meet this week, and keep sending stamped return envelopes, they are bound get the hint and write back. (If not, feel free to write a hint in capital letters.) Writing is a lost skill. With a little perseverance, you can bring it back.

Seeing Is Believing. If you have a videotape recorder, you can send your grandchildren home movie messages. Ask a friend to be your camera operator. Or set up the camera somewhere, wave your arms, and talk a lot. Or you could videotape a walking tour while you talk, then hold out the camera, turn it around, and give them a kiss goodbye.

Letters by Ear. Audio tapes can be even more fun, because they are less threatening. It's not such a big deal. You won't be required to brush your hair or clean the room for your tape recorder. Just press "record" and start talking. Keep a running list of entertaining topics right next to your grocery list.

Younger children will love hearing your voice, no matter what you are saying. Teenagers will think your "audio letter" is cool and listen to you while they procrastinate studying. Or they can play your tape in the car when the radio has too many commercials.

A tape can be heard by anyone, regardless of who it is intended for, so your grandchild might enjoy hiding out or listening in privacy with headphones. In fact, inexpensive headphones would make a good birthday gift. Encourage your grandchild to record his response and any additional ramblings right over your message on the same tape. You can use cardboard audio tape mailers and label them TOP SECRET or FOR YOUR EARS ONLY to make them a really big deal.

Keep in touch!

You know you're a grandma when ...

— you buy film in multipacks.

— your children start listening to your opinions.

— you reschedule all your appointments around your grandchildren's visit.

— you know who Baby Bop is.

13

How Your Lifestyle Affects Your Role

Age doesn't protect you from love.
But love, to some extent, does protect you from age.
— Jeanne Moreau

Picture Marlene Dietrich on the cover of Life magazine in August 1948. A sultry siren, the ultimate femme ... would you believe "Grandmother Dietrich"? That's what they called her, and so she was. Having grandchildren enhanced her version of the older, sexual female. It added classic beauty to the Grandma Hall of Fame. In fact, Ms. Dietrich disguised herself in a nurse uniform to stroll with her grandson through Central Park. She bought her daughter a brownstone and lived in a Park Avenue hotel until she found a suitable home nearby. In interviews, she explained that she worked to take care of her family. A woman extraordinaire? No, just your average, everyday grandma.

After all, what do Barbara Bush, Whoopi Goldberg, Priscilla Presley, and Raquel Welch have in common with you? You guessed it: grandchildren! Which proves that grandmothers come in every size, color, style, and shape. As long as your arms fit around the baby, you are perfect.

Single Grandmas

Men die younger than women do. It's a fact. Consequently, quite a few single grandmas are out there. Divorce multiplies the situation. Some grandmas never married. As any grandma will attest, grandchildren go a long way to fill up a single grandma's heart.

If you have a boyfriend, that's terrific. But, don't let him come between you and your grandchildren. You might both enjoy visiting your grandchildren separately. If you want to bring him along on your visits or include him at your place, fine. Just be sure to focus your attention on the kids. They're the "sure thing"!

Stepgrandmas

If you are a new stepgrandma, dive right in. More people to love equals more people to love you back. Try not to have any expectations — you may not be welcomed with tiny open arms. Accept that the children might be nervous with you. Just remember, the way to a man's heart isn't only through his stomach! If you initiate a real relationship with his grandchildren everyone will benefit. If you can't stand the kids, be comforted that you had nothing to do with them getting that way. However, you can have something to do with making them nicer.

If you have married a widower, you are desperately needed to fulfill the grandma role, whether the children consciously realize this or not. If you married a divorcé, you can help him maintain or reestablish a good relationship with his grandchildren. In every case, be consistently supportive. When you accept the responsibilities of being a grandma, all the benefits will be yours as well.

My stepgrandma came into my life when my real grandma was alive and flourishing, so we naturally called our grandfather's wife by her first name. Twenty years later, my hand hesitates each time I write that name on a letter to her and my grandfather. She has always been supportive, loving, generous — and a real kick to be around. She has always made an effort to connect with me by spending time alone with me or with my family and she has succeeded. She never tried to replace my grandma; she is unique in her own way. She is truly a grandma.

"Step" doesn't have to be a four-letter word. You can bring joy to many lives, including your own.

Remarried Grandmas

It's perfectly acceptable to visit your grandchildren without your husband. Maybe you will each visit your respective grandchildren at the same time. However, if you spend time with your grandchildren as a team, be sure you get equal time. If you were single for awhile, you may have had many impromptu visits from your grandchildren. That's less likely to happen now, so plan ahead. If your husband doesn't have grandchildren, don't let him keep you away. On the contrary, teach him how the relationship works. He'll learn to appreciate your methods and you. Remember, your grandchildren will always be there for you as long as you are always there for them. Have an influence on the future — and a good time as well!

Adopted Grandmas

A grandma is a grandma is a grandma. Unconditional love takes patience and understanding. Contribute to the warm environment that will make your grandchild feel secure. Years from now, when the child has natural doubts about his adopted parents versus his genetic parents, your role in his life will not be questioned. You will always be grandma.

Surrogate Moms

You may have finished raising your children, only to find yourself raising your children's children. This is not unusual. If you are the one who keeps track of when and what the children eat, then face it — you're the mother. With your wisdom and relaxed attitude about child rearing, the children are lucky to have you. Times do change, so keeping up with current child development theories is vital! Don't despair. Turn on the television to T. Berry Brazelton and Penelope Leach's parenting shows. Read the current parenting books and magazines — you'll be amazed at how helpful they can be. Though your energy may flag, your great emotional expertise will serve you well. The children need you. They'll appreciate you more than you'll ever know. You may not be all fun and games, but you'll be one cherished grandma.

What's Your Style?

Around the country, women are lining up to be grandmas. It's the latest craze! Indeed, there are almost as many kinds of grandmas as there are women. Let's see if you can find your type.

East Coast Grandma

Dress: Always in stockings or grey flannel trousers, the ultimate in sophistication, she has a standing appointment at the hairdresser.

On Hearing the News: Gets a certified illustration of the family tree, matted and framed, and hangs it in the foyer.

Gifts: Mock Chanel suits and manicure kits to the girls; suspenders and hockey sticks to the boys.

Playtime: The American Museum of Natural History for the dinosaur exhibit; Carnegie Hall for the children's matinee.

Baby Blanket: Handmade in Europe or Hackensack.

Breakfast: Croissants or bagels with fresh-squeezed orange juice.

Favorites: Loves to be compared to a mother duck with her adorable ducklings following her all in a line.

West Coast Grandma

Dress: Usually blonde, she wears dangling earrings the baby loves to play with and revels in leggings and oversized T-shirts.

On Hearing the News: Installs a child's seat on her bicycle.

Gifts: Mickey Mouse T-shirts, bright-colored sunblock, Boogie Boards, and Frisbees.

Playtime: Finger painting and collecting seashells.

Baby Blanket: Only the best for baby — Baby Dior from the local department store.

Breakfast: Fruit salad and seven-grain toast.

Favorites: Loves to be mistaken for the children's mother.

Southwest Grandma

Dress: Silver and turquoise jewelry, espadrilles, and jeans.

On Hearing the News: Has the air conditioning fixed, finally, for the baby's visit.

Gifts: Moccasins, cowboy hats, and board games.

Playtime: "I Spy" during sunrise walks.

Blanket: Woven Native American papoose blanket from the nearby reservation.

Breakfast: Pozoles and scrambled eggs.

Favorites: Loves to sketch her grandchildren in oil pastels.

Southern Grandma

Dress: Has five pairs of white pants, keeps hair short or pulled back with a ribbon, and wears novelty earrings in the shape of alligators and cows.

On Hearing the News: Calls on all the neighbors bringing home-made jam.

Gifts: Sundresses with matching hats and jump ropes for girls, sneakers and fishing rods for boys.

Playtime: Gardening and card games.

Baby Blanket: Baby-sized quilt made with friends.

Breakfast: Sunny-side-up eggs and hominy grits.

Favorites: Loves to take them to town and introduce them everywhere.

Northern Grandma

Dress: Monogrammed sweater and penny loafers with nickels in them, same hairdo since college (usually pageboy).

On Hearing the News: Starts putting together a care package of baby toiletries and digs out the family christening gown.

Gifts: Orders monogrammed jumpers from catalogs, matching mittens-and-hat sets for everyone, plus box kites such as the ones she had when she was a girl.

Playtime: Hide-and-seek and watching The Wizard of Oz.

Blanket: Hand knit by the fire.

Breakfast: Oatmeal, fresh blueberry muffins, and frozen juice.

Favorites: Loves family gatherings — plans for Thanksgiving all year round.

Midwest Grandma

Dress: Gray hair and designer warm-up suit.

On Hearing the News: Holds neighborhood brunch to announce news publicly.

Gifts: Big Ten sweatshirts, red wagons, and sleds.

Playtime: Feeding the animals and reading books at bedtime.

Blanket: Hand-crocheted during All My Children.

Breakfast: Fresh pancakes with lots of sausage.

Favorites: Loves to have everybody in matching red, white, and blue outfits on the Fourth of July.

How Do Your Grandchildren See You?

To see how your grandchildren view you, ask them to draw you a picture. As the saying goes, a picture really is worth a thousand words.

Children are first capable of drawing faces between the ages of three and four. Once the young artists mature and their hand-eye coordination is honed, they learn to add more details. Nevertheless, arms, legs, eyelashes, and clothing will not change the essence of your portrait. The differences between the artwork of one child and another depends less on each child's specific talents and more on how each child understands the subject ... how they see you in their mind's eye. The real contrast between two children's portraits will be determined by your relationship.

Ideally, your face will be full and round. Your eyes will be open and your mouth will be smiling. It doesn't matter if you have a body or not, as long as you fill most of the page. When this child thinks of you, you are the center of the universe. If you are on the left side of the page, the child has a strong attachment to you, but draws your likeness from a hazy memory. Your image is likely borrowed from grandmothers in books or on television. If your picture is very small or your face is in profile, the relationship has little to draw on — literally. Sometimes a child will draw a doll or a puppet figure with old-fashioned clothes and no expression. This means the child can only imagine grandma. It's time to pick up the phone.

As an experiment, I asked Juliette to draw a picture of Grandma Claire. Her hair was yellow, her face was a huge circle with round eyes and a U-shaped smile. Next, I asked her to draw a picture of Grandma Jean. Juliette only met Grandma Jean once, when she was a tiny infant. She sees the family photograph of Grandma Jean holding her when we lift her up in the hallway to look. She has also seen pictures in our scrapbook. She knows Grandma Jean has been in Heaven for a long time now. Since this relationship was so brief, I expected a pretend grandma in the picture. She asked me what Grandma Jean's hair looked like, then proceeded to draw another big happy face. Scrambling, I called my mother.

She assured me the studies were still accurate. Because Juliette has a good relationship with her, and all the data she has received about Grandma Jean has been positive as well, that relationship has been validated in her mind through memories and photographs. Juliette has no reason to have any empty or negative feelings about her late grandmother.

So, according to my expert, Juliette reinforced the conclusions by illustrating that a positive relationship with one grandmother can influence her feelings about grandmothers in general.

Psychologists use pictures a great deal when working with young children. They concentrate on the children's ability to develop small motor ability to draw recognizable forms, rather than on the picture's style or content. In other words, children are not sophisticated enough to fabricate an image. Their pictures don't lie. So, don't ask for a portrait unless you truly want one. If you get a big happy face, frame it!

Just Grandma

Do you ever feel pressured about being Super Grandma? Concerned that your true talents might not fit the bill? Or exhausted already from trying to be this woman? Don't worry, Super Grandma is a hard image to live up to. In fact it's impossible — and unnecessary.

Face it, you are incredibly talented at a number things. But not everything. Fortunately, you don't have to be the best at everything. You don't even have to try everything. Remember that old adage, "jack-of-all-trades, master of none"? You undoubtedly have your share of talents. After all, you have other things in your life besides your role as a grandmother. Many of these things will add zest to the love you have to offer your grandchildren.

Perfection is not the goal — neither for you nor for your grandchild. You don't have to teach manners, ballroom dancing, and

French. Don't try so hard to know all things, teach all things, and be all things—simply offer what you know. The goal is to have a good relationship. Relax and enjoy each other.

Most people have a treasured memory of one special time spent with grandma. My mother's friend Suzanne yearns to return to that summer afternoon when she sang songs while her grandma brushed her hair. She remembers being told how her hair shone and how beautifully she sang. She remembers feeling that her grandmother would have loved her hair and her singing no matter what — because her grandma loved her no matter what. She felt especially close to her grandma that day and realized that she loved her grandma no matter what, as well.

When asked about their favorite memories of grandparents, adult grandchildren have similar answers in almost every case. They relive time spent just relaxing and talking with their grandparents, getting to know them ... and getting to love them. (This may explain why fishing is so popular.) What is your favorite memory of your grandma? What do you want your grandchildren to remember? You? Share yourself.

Nature Versus Nurture

Nature's role is predetermined. Those chromosomes are pretty darned influential. In fact, if you have a daughter, your genetic power is even clearer: her baby's genes were partially formed while she was inside you. In addition, you have another role that is at least as important—the role of nurturer.

What comes to mind when you think of the word "grandma"? The old-fashioned vision of a soft, aproned woman, stirring a steaming pot and removing a sheet of sticky buns from the oven? Maybe that doesn't describe you — but it is, believe it or not, what you're all about.

The greatest human needs are food, clothing, and shelter. Notice the order these fall in. Food is number one. Food equals love, especially to children. Food shouldn't replace love, or this confusion could lead to eating disorders. So, perhaps we should consider food as an accessory to love. After all, romance is usually sparked by a candle-light dinner, *n'est ce pas?* Food is the easiest and most obvious way to express your love. It provides sustenance of the most basic sort. Therefore, this traditional stereotype of grandmother in the kitchen is not a threat to you. On the contrary, it reinforces your very essence. Consequently, the kitchen is an honorable place.

Although legendary family dinners may be a relic of our collective past, you can still feed your grandchildren. If you don't like to cook, so what? A child won't care that lack of cooking time is the reason your cupboard is bare. He'll only see that his friends' grandmas feed them and you don't feed him. So, in his mind, you must not love him.

Fulfilling this minimum requirement for grandmothers is easy: keep your cupboards stocked. As long as you have some version of Cheerios, apple juice, chocolate pudding, and hugs, your grandchildren will know you to be the Great Nurturer. You can be a legend in your own time.

You know you're a grandma when ...

— you dress in green because it's your grandchild's favorite color.

— you are paying for ballet lessons — again.

— your daughter wants to visit (with the kids).

— you'd rather dine with a three-year-old than with an eligible bachelor.

— you know why little girls are named Ariel, Belle, and Jasmine.

14

How to Have a Happy Visit

*A grandmother is a babysitter
who watches the kids instead of television.*
— Anonymous child, age six

Your Home

If your first reaction to becoming a grandparent was fear for the sanctity of your home, don't despair. Go ahead, pack up all your crystal and everything else that's breakable, valuable, sentimental, small, sharp, or poisonous. Cover your couches with blanket throws, indefinitely postpone the white Berber carpet, and put that Architectural Digest back on the bookshelf. In fact, maybe you should fear for the sanctity of your home!

It wasn't until I had my first baby that I understood why my paternal grandmother's furniture was always covered in plastic.

Plastic was everywhere in the sixties, so I had assumed it was some kind of a fashion statement. Other grandparents were famous for their creative use of slip covers. If these ideas sound like a good way to save your furniture, be sure you know what it is you are saving the furniture for. In any case, if you plan on having your grandchildren around, either the place will have to change or your designer dreams will.

Baby-proof for the baby's safety and kid-proof for your own peace of mind. Then take a deep breath and expect the worst. Reality may be terrifyingly close, but at least you'll be relaxed about it. If you're too nervous to enjoy the children, then the children will be nervous, too. After all, nobody likes to hang out daily at a museum—it's great for short, formal visits, but there's no place comfortable to sit, you can't touch anything past your nose (and even that is frowned on), and you certainly can't bring your lunch. You want your grand-children to visit, so you'll adapt. After only another fifteen years, you can unpack that Ming vase. Think how much more it will be worth then.

Here are some specific tips to help both you and the kids feel at home:

Keep some toys on hand. Nothing big or expensive, just some generic stuff to keep the children busy during the ten minutes before dinner when they're bored with the twenty-eight toys they brought with them. Animal puppets are great because you can get involved — this little bit of effort goes a long way in the children's estimation of grandma. No need to try to be a ventriloquist for children under ten — they are more interested in your imagination than your method. Crayons and paper are a perennial favorite because children can play by themselves, and you can always assign them a particular picture to extend the activity. Puzzles and some type of colorful building blocks are a safe bet. (Be sure to avoid pieces smaller than one-and-a-half inches for children under age three.) Best of all, a six- to eight-inch ball will be popular with every age group and will also help get the whole brood out of the house for a little while.

Stop at the video store before your grandchildren's arrival. Get some wholesome cartoons or a suitable family movie to help fill those restless hours before bedtime. Never trust the ratings labels on movies! Many popular movies marketed for children have strong language and violence. Even though the the kids may watch a certain movie at their house, parents aren't always completely aware of the contents. More importantly, it doesn't mean grandma has to condone it. To discover other options, ask the clerk in the store. Better yet, now might be the perfect time to meet the young parents down the block.

Visit the library and check out some fun books. The librarian can help you find appropriate choices. Plenty of books have stories about grandmas, too! They will serve as tools for quiet time as well as for quality time when you read together.

Don't spend too much time cleaning up before the big visit. The sparkling visage of clean rooms won't last long, and you'll just have to clean again when they leave. If the visit is short and you have gifts for the children that don't fall into the clothing category, save one as a reward for helping you clean up. That way they'll spend the precious hours of the visit focusing on you, not just on the new toys — and they'll have something fresh and exciting to remember you by.

If you have time to shop for groceries, find out what the kids like to eat. Now is not the time to train them to eat properly. Sure, have some vegetables and dip as a fun, healthy alternative. But if they really love macaroni and cheese for dinner, don't bother with liver and onions. It's not worth the effort or the smell. Remind the parents to bring the multivitamins or keep some handy. Keep spaghetti and other easy meals on hand. Taking the crowd out to eat takes twice as much time, money, discipline, discomfort, and laundry.

You do not have to clear your schedule completely. If the visit is for several days, invite the kids along to your tennis game. Suggest alternative activities while you use those theater tickets you ordered months ago. Bring your grandson and his new book with you to the hairdresser and then take him to the train exhibit. Let your granddaughter have a manicure. Visit that sick friend during nap time (if the kids' parents are there to watch them). Have your out-of-town friend visit you for a half hour. Children need to respect that grandma has a life too, but they need to know that even with all your activities, your favorite time is with them.

If possible, keep a high chair and crib at your place for overnight visitors. Owning those necessary pieces of furniture is a heck of a lot easier than bringing them, renting them, or not having them — and it might lead to more frequent visits. Discount stores have lots of baby sales. The new high chairs are padded, easy to clean, and fold up nicely to fit in the closet. You may find great deals at garage sales and consignment stores, but be wary. Always keep safety standards in mind when buying used baby equipment — even from friends. Don't get anything damaged or old. Safety standards are updated constantly as accidents are reported. Go to the library and read Consumer Reports or call the manufacturer's customer service department.

Always use car seats! Not only are they required by law, but in fatal traffic accidents, the infant in the car seat is usually the one who survives. Most accidents happen on the home stretch — when you're tired and your guard is down because home is just around the corner. Always use car seats! Many infants have been killed while in their mothers' arms on the way to the emergency room.

This is the biggest challenge with Grandma Claire. When she was a young mother, there were no car seat laws. But there was less traffic then and perhaps less accurate accident statistics. Her initial protests against car seats don't justify the danger. Make it a habit to use infant seats, booster seats, and seat belts — but no air bags! Air bags can be very dangerous to small children. The tremendous force of inflation is ideal for the average adult test dummy, but very harmful for children. Infants have been badly hurt when air bags crushed their infant seats. Until carmakers improve these safety features, have the children sit in appropriate safety seats and use appropriate seat belts in the back seat.

Never leave children unattended. Not when you run into the dry cleaners, not when the phone rings, never! Take the kids with you. Use safety straps. Count on the worst. Newborns can squirm and fall out of infant seats. Babies can choke just resting on your bed. Toddlers drown in bathtubs and toilets — it really happens. Ten-year-olds can find that loose nail — in their foot. Teenagers can slice their fingers instead of sandwiches. It pays to be paranoid!

Their Home

Keep an open mind. The experts say if a house where a toddler lives is immaculate, something is terribly amiss. People are more important than things. If you can't stand the mess — or if the mess is more than simple clutter — ask before you roll up your sleeves and clean up. Uninvited cleaning may be taken as an insult. Be a blessing, not a burden. Smile and be glad it's not your place.

Gifts are not required. If you can't resist bringing your grandchild a gift, try to avoid sweets. Parents have enough trouble controlling children's nutritional intake. If you can't think of anything spectacular, but don't want to show up empty-handed, bring fun and useful items such as bubble-blowing solution, sidewalk chalk, or character toothbrushes. Think educational with a fun twist, like musical or pop-up books.

If you can't resist that adorable pinafore or the athletic shoes with blinking lights, leave the tags on them. Offer the parents the receipts. A child can stay dormant for months and then grow an inch in twenty-four hours! The children may not fit in the clothes, they may already have these items, or they may be in dire need of something else. For teenagers, money is always appreciated. If you give them five dollars, let them to spend it on themselves and have fun. If you give them twenty dollars, talk to them about saving up for that new bike. That way, your gift is a lesson in disguise.

Participate in activities with them. Get down on the floor and roll the ball to the baby, make animals out of clay alongside the toddler, play dolls, or color with the school children. Sneak in a little fresh air and exercise by asking the older children to take a walk with you and show you where their friends live, or take a "listening" walk where you describe the sounds you hear and what makes them. Influence good reading habits by reading stories to them, taking them to the library, and buying them special-interest magazines and, yes, even comic books. Plan a big event for your visit that everyone can look forward to and remember when you are gone. For the little ones, this may mean a simple park outing; the older ones may be anxious to see the new Disney movie or visit the harvest festival. You don't have to take them places by yourself — you just have to be there to share the experience.

Baby-sitting can be fun. For the parents, for the children, and — yes! — even for you. Be sure to get a list of do's and don'ts: remember the safety rules, then ignore the rest! Knowing you are breaking the rules is a lot more fun than winging it.

With older kids, lay down your own ground rules for peace of mind. Then offer freedom within that structure. Be an accomplice — let them stay up late and order pizza! No harm will be done and the parents will be so grateful for the free night, late-sleeping, and happy kids. They won't complain a bit. They probably expected it, anyway.

You know you're a grandma when ...

— you give carpet-cleaning liquid as a gift to your grand-mother friends.

— you look forward to ballet recitals.

— you install a crib in your den.

— you have popsicles in your freezer.

— you primp more for your grandchildren than you do for your husband.

15

Special Events: Activities, Meals, and Vacations

Being grandparents sufficiently removes us from the responsibilities so that we can be friends — really good friends.
— Dr. Allan Frome, pediatrician

Every occasion with grandma is a special one. The best way to make events particularly special is to make a tradition of doing them with you.

If you live nearby, you can join a Mommy and Me class with the baby and make it your regular — special — outing. You can be the one who takes the kids to the new G-rated film each time one opens. You can take them to dancing or martial arts lessons.

If you live far away from your grandchildren, how about planning ahead for the ball game, the concert in the park, or even the circus? At our house, Grandma Claire takes the girls to McDonalds for breakfast. Juliette calls it "Ol' McDonalds" and Catherine calls it "E-yi-e-yi-o," so they have a tradition of singing all the way there. After eating, they run wild in the restaurant playground.

When we're at grandma's, Juliette and Grandma Claire's special event is feeding the ducks at the nearby pond. Sometimes, the rest of the family joins them. When grandma is busy, I take Juliette to the pond. But I'm just a visitor — duck feeding is their thing, the special event that Juliette associates with grandma. And this association is what always makes it so special.

Whether it's twice a year or twice a month, as long as you share the activity on a consistent basis, almost anything will fit the bill.

Family Dining

Do you love to eat out? If so, you'll naturally want to go out with your growing clan. Here's a typical scenario: at first, you'll play Queen Mum and pay for everyone. This is a generous attitude and you'll all have a wonderful time. By the second time, the credit card bill for the first meal will have arrived, and you might be a tad less enthusiastic. Your son-in-law will probably be anxious to pay this time, but you'll overrule him and say it's your pleasure. By the third time, you will be reluctant to mention eating out and will be grateful when your daughter suggests you all go out "on them."

If you eat out with the family regularly and wish to settle the uncomfortable issue of paying, establish an understanding that everyone will pay their own way. Simply state that you (and your husband) will contribute your share.

Another eating-out-related issue is the grandchildren's lack of knowledge about restaurant etiquette. When you take the grandchildren out to eat, don't expect them to behave like little adults — they are not. Bring toys, crayons, and patience. Avoid going at naptime and bedtime. Teach them about restaurant etiquette at a level they can understand and achieve. Plan a tour of the restaurant to stretch those little legs and burn off some of the energy that would drive everyone crazy if it stayed pent-up in the booth.

Family meals at home can be a struggle as well. If you can, offer to help with groceries at their house, but do take "no" for an answer. For a meal at your house, asking them to pick up something specific, like beverages and dessert or a fresh flower centerpiece is easier than divvying up the cost of a large family meal. Money is not a dirty word as long as you keep it out in the open. Once you can talk about it, you'll all have more fun, and bartering for clean-up chores may be acceptable to everyone.

Vacations
With the Family

A friend of mine, Kim, had the good fortune to go to Hawaii on vacation this year. She took along her thirteen-year-old babysitter to help with the three children, all under four. I was green with envy. She agreed that the situation was pretty good, but then she told me about a family on the plane who really vacationed in style. The parents enjoyed the luxury of first class, while their housekeeper dealt with the kids in coach. To me, this was beyond a good idea — it was fantasy land.

The possibilities for a perfect vacation simmered in my mind for several days. I planned how I would do it and what the perfect conditions would entail. I thought about what babysitter I would bring. Could she be trusted in a strange place? How much time off would she need? Wouldn't she just be another child to be responsible for? Would we be comfortable living with her for a week? We'd have to pay for her trip and expenses — how much salary would we have to pay? I thought about it and thought about it.

If the children were older, we could solve the vacation riddle by going to a hotel with a children's activity schedule. But for now the situation seemed desperate. Then it dawned on me. My mother fit all my requirements, met all my concerns — and would be more fun.

Plus, she'd enjoy the vacation.

Hawaii was out of the question. Instead, we decided to drive down to La Jolla, near San Diego, for a long weekend. Mom was raring to go. She offered to pay for her room and we quickly agreed to pay for everything else. We got adjoining rooms — guess who the kids wanted to sleep with? The first few days were blissful. We played on the beach together, took turns doing whatever we were in the mood for, and someone always wanted to go inside while the baby napped. My husband and I went out to dinner by ourselves and took romantic walks on the beach. The children were safe and happy. And even if we felt like being grumpy, we could do it without always trying to put on a happy face for a stranger. We took advantage of Grandma Claire — without taking advantage of her. She gave us breathing room. When grandma got sick of us, she took a long walk and disappeared for three hours. By the time she returned, she was refreshed and we were starting to miss her. I admit, the arrangement wasn't ideal all the time, but it was close.

A few days later, I overheard my husband telling a friend about our vacation. "That's right, my mother-in-law," he said, "My motto is 'Grandma Claire: don't leave home without her!'"

The moral of the story is, volunteer to go on vacation with your grandchildren. If you are married or involved, you'll need to work out the logistics with your mate. Either way, keep these points in mind: you're better than a babysitter, you'll share a memorable experience with the children, and you might get a free vacation out of it.

Without the Family

Grandma Claire dreams of taking the girls on world cruises with her. She wants to travel the Orient, visit the Louvre, and relax in the Caribbean with her granddaughters. She wants to share the world with them. Maybe you sent your children to Europe or the Grand Canyon. Wouldn't you rather take them?

Vacationing with your grandchildren can be a wonderful experience. They are away from parental pressures and so are you. You have a constant companion who looks up to you and follows your lead. You can revisit places with a fresh perspective. You can explore new places as you never imagined them. Or you can relax and enjoy your grandchild's company in a fun environment where bedtimes don't matter and you don't have to make the beds.

Most resort hotels now offer children's programs, so you don't have to be responsible for twenty-four-hour entertainment. You can have both a good time and meet new friends. The Los Angeles Times recently devoted the entire travel section to family cruises, available from many of the cruise lines. The RFD Travel Corporation offers tour packages specifically for grandparents and grandchildren (age eight to sixteen) to explore America together. Not only can you rediscover your heritage, but you can personally introduce your heirs to their ancestors. Visit your travel agent or call the Auto Club and map out your own road trip. Plan a vacation that you and your grandchild will never forget!

You know you're a grandma when ...

— strange children talk to you in public places.

— your son considers you an authority.

— your favorite jewelry is plastic.

— you love home movies.

16

Family Politics

Who takes a child by the hand
takes the mother by the heart.
— Danish proverb

Did you marry for love? If you are royalty, then probably not. In fact, most marriages before this century were planned by people who had ulterior motives for uniting individuals. Lives were arranged to further business and political pursuits. The union of two people could ally opposing clans. The birth of a baby could prevent a war.

Even now, a new baby can bring a family together in peace. You can be the facilitator. You don't have to declare the winner of historical disagreements, or even negotiate a truce. Simply ignore the strained communications and start a peaceful new era. A grandchild gives relatives something in common: someone new has their blood. Let your enthusiasm for the new baby draw the family close.

Extended Family

Send birth announcements! If the proud parents are spreading the news, put your order in for a dozen additional cards. Tempt them with the likelihood of more gifts by reminding them to get thank-you notes as well. Offer to do the family announcements, or to help with all the addresses. Some mothers like to write all the cards alone as a rite of passage — it makes a personal situation real in terms of the outside world. Most parents will be so overwhelmed — especially with the first child — that they'll welcome your help.

Last week, I received an announcement from an old friend whose baby was born ten days earlier. I was amazed how fast Lisa accomplished the social niceties. When I called, her mother-in-law answered the phone. I knew they had a respectfully distant relationship. Lisa picked up the phone and explained how her mother-in-law was so excited about the baby that she flew in without her husband, rolled up her sleeves, and got to work. Her mother-in-law had sent out the announcements! It was the start of a new relationship for all of them. It doesn't matter who pays for the postage or where the postmarks are stamped, this is a fun way to be helpful.

On a Sunday, soon after the announcements are mailed, get out your phone book. People will be relaxed at the end of a weekend — and the phone rates will be low. Feel free to call cousins you haven't heard from in years. No one can cast doubt on the excitement of a grandmother — no matter how many grandchildren you have. Every grandchild is special and worthy of celebration. Mention how the baby's chin reminds you of them. Offer to send a photograph. Ask for phone numbers and addresses of others — for more announcements or for your Christmas card list. Even remote relatives are bound to feel more connected. Once you are in touch, you decide whether to stay in touch. At least, make the first effort. Maybe one day soon they'll call you.

In-Laws and Outlaws

Now is a good time to get to know your married children's in-laws. You are bound to be thrown together on family occasions from here on out — why not get to know each other first? Holidays are stressful times even when relationships are smooth; you can make them go that much smoother by eliminating the additional challenge of getting along with the in-laws. Relatives are given, not chosen, and in this case the only thing you may have in common is your children. Inviting them for coffee or a commemorative glass of champagne will initiate a new relationship that may offer you things you never would have imagined. At least make the effort. If the get-together doesn't work out so well, maybe it's because they are shy or afraid. Maybe they just need more time. What do you have to lose? Nothing. On the contrary, you'll have gained the edge for those grandchildren's birthday parties. You'll be able to smile easy. After all, you tried.

Competition is healthy in many arenas, but the family is not one of them. Avoid forcing your children to choose between your house and the in-laws' house for Thanksgiving. Offer an alternative holiday — or ask if you can join them. When you have many family members to consider, it helps to plan ahead.

Competing over grandchildren can get nasty. The fact that your in-laws bought the playhouse doesn't mean you have to splurge for a swing set. This is not a contest for the affection of your grandchildren. Go along with the program. Buy a child-sized chair for the playhouse. How about a plastic phone or rake? Children don't keep score. Often, little ones enjoy playing with the boxes more than the gifts. You may find that a simple jump rope will turn out to be the favored toy — despite the expense of more extravagant gifts. The only element that will truly make a difference to the grandchildren is the time you spend with them. This, however, is not a competition. It's a joy!

Daughters and Sons

Oh, my son's my son 'til he gets him a wife,
but my daughter's my daughter all her life.
— D. Craik

If your daughter has a child you are lucky, indeed. Regardless of your previous relationship, a door has opened between you. Now she can understand where you are coming from — or at least where you started. Now you are the undeniable expert. It's the ideal opportunity to become friends. Mothers and daughters classically have their highs and lows. My mother and I were no exception. Everything has changed now. Not only do we have motherhood in common, but also we both want the best for my children.

If your son has a child, you also have an opportunity to be close to him. He'll probably appreciate you more now that he knows what you went through for him. Take advantage!

Either way, shower that baby with all the love and affection you have to offer. Don't wait for your son's or daughter's invitation for anything — except advice. Just because you decked out your child in fancy clothes doesn't mean they are appropriate for your grandchild — even baby fashions change. Keep your relationship alive by being clear with your children about visiting hours. The rest is easy.

No one can resist another person who loves their baby. Your child will be able to see you from a whole new perspective. He or she will enjoy the view ... and you will gain easy access to your grandchild.

Sons-in-Law

Fathers have become a luxury item in our society. If you have a son-in-law, especially one who lives with your grandchildren, count your blessings. He is very important to your grandchildren's well-being. If he is gone, you are likely to become his replacement. It's best for the children to have you both.

Make friends ... it's easier than you think. If your daughter is like you in any respect, then he will automatically relate to that part of you. If she is like his mother, then you must be a bit like his mother, as well.

If you can't put your finger on anything remotely similar between the three of you, relax. Perhaps you are relatively close in age and have some history in common. Perhaps you share a bit of geography. It could be that you have a mutual interest in some hobby.

In my family, both my husband and my mother are well read. They are also well-versed in movie trivia. She prefers romances to his westerns, but it makes no difference. My husband doesn't really care who is the director's daughter by whom or by which marriage, but he almost always knows. My mother sometimes calls him up to verify her stories or to point out something about an old movie that's appearing on television. The other day, she called to discuss the original filming of Silas Marner. She thought she'd surprise him with some new information, but he knew even more than she did. They connect.

The least common denominator in your relationship with your son-in-law is also the greatest: the grandchildren. No matter what aggravation may arise between you, the relationship will forge ahead because you are both crazy about the children. If your son-in-law happens to be one of those unusual fathers who has trouble relating to, or truly appreciating, young children, you can help. Get him involved by asking where those cute ears came from. Request to see his baby pictures. Asking a man about himself is the closest thing to outright flattery. You can't make it any easier for him to like you than when you compare the baby's spunky character or twinkling eyes to the father's.

You don't have to be equals to be friends with your son-in-law. In fact, you really can't be pals on that level. You are the superior being. You did give birth to the woman he loves, after all. Without you, his little bundle of joy wouldn't be here. Give your son-in-law the chance to treat you with respect. Let him know how you expect to be treated by acting in a manner that deserves respect.

Let your presence in your son-in-law's life be a positive one. Send him birthday cards. Have one of his favorite foods on hand when he visits. (My mother usually stocks up on pistachio ice cream.) Be patient. Your daughter can help, but only you can make this relationship work.

Daughters-in-Law

She wants to love you! She may not know it, but loving you would make her life so much easier — and a lot more fun. As the grandmother, you have a lot of power. Use it to empower your daughter-in-law. She will be grateful and you will end up where you started — powerful.

Your goal is to be the consummate grandmother. Never lose sight of this objective, which relies a great deal on your relationship with this woman. You don't have to be crazy about your daughter-in-law, but give her the benefit of the doubt. Watch her with your son and your grandchild. You might come to like her a lot.

My mother's friend Eileen never felt close to her daughter-in-law. Jill was a modern young wife, open in her concern about how a child would interfere with her busy career and social life. The relationship between Eileen and her daughter-in-law could best be described as reserved — and reserved for holidays. For several years this coolness didn't seem to matter. However, since the baby was born the two women have realized that they are more alike than different. More than anything else, they love the same man and his baby. They are working partners in their family's life.

The easiest way to get your daughter-in-law to like you is to let her know you are on her team. If you can, take her to lunch while she's pregnant or for her first time out with the baby. Tell her you are on her side — then follow through. Help make life easier for her.

Let your daughter-in-law set the pace. If she doesn't know you very well, let her see how you respond to her beloved baby. Show her how much you love that little tyke. Even if you raised four children, ask her opinion about which baby bonnet she would prefer you to buy. Bring her a frozen casserole so she doesn't have to cook. Offer to watch the baby while she takes a nap or gets her hair cut. Rent a video or take a class in CPR to assure her that you care enough to be a safe babysitter. Most importantly, let her know that you would love to help, within reason.

If she doesn't want your assistance, give her some space. Offer it for another time. Her reserved demeanor doesn't mean she's a snob or she doesn't like you. It probably means she is shy or nervous about not knowing how to please you. Maybe she imagines that you are hovering close, watching to see if she's a good mother. That's enough to make anyone insecure, self-conscious, and clumsy. Who knows what your husband told her about you? Possibly very little. Tell her about yourself. Tell her about your son and what it was like being his mother. Describing what her baby's father was like as a baby is a sure icebreaker.

Since you value this relationship, you're easy to take advantage of. If she asks too much of you, gently tell her you're not available. Set limits. You'll both be much happier if you know exactly where you stand. Let it be a two-way street. Encourage your daughter-in-law to kick you out when you've overstayed your welcome. Phrase your suggestion in a way that seems polite: ask her to let you know when she wants some privacy.

If you are at your daughter-in-law's house and notice she's getting irritable, suggest that you should be going. Make up some errand. If she is reluctant, maybe what she really needs is a ten-minute nap. If she doesn't respond, skedaddle. Wouldn't you rather be gone than resented? That baby has a lot of birthdays coming up — you want to be invited!

You know you're a grandma when ...

— you want to move next door to your daughter.

— your old clothes are back in style.

— you'll do anything to stop your grandchild's tears.

— everything the children do is wonderful, brilliant, or adorable.

— you know about the new Little Tykes merchandise before your local toy store does.

17

Dealing
with Divorce

*God could not be everywhere so he created parents,
and when they became too busy he created grandparents.*
— Sunie Levin, author

The "D" word is everywhere. You can try to explain the infinite advantages of commitment and the immeasurable tragedies of divorce. You can offer your own experience as an example. You can even suggest counseling. Once you've contributed this sage advice, step back and stay out of it.

Should this marriage be worked out? Should it be ended? It affects you, your child, and your grandchildren. It is entirely your business ... yet it is none of your business. Even though a divorce is public, it is deeply personal. Resist the temptation. Be supportive, but do not get involved. There is too much private history you don't know and too many intimate details that you will never know. Logic rarely prevails over emotions. Your interference will make you an enemy in both camps.

Worst of all, divorce can make sustaining a close relationship with your grandchildren difficult. Don't give up! Those kids need you now more than ever. Regardless of how many of their friends' parents are divorced or how well they seem to be taking it, the pain is there and it will manifest itself someday.

Today's young adults are the first generation that are as likely to have been raised in broken homes as not. Divorce is so prevalent that even the term "broken home" seems antiquated. "Dysfunctional family" is a term that is liberally applied. Just because divorce is common, however, doesn't mean it should be condoned. We have to think about the children.

During a recent visit, Juliette told Grandma Claire a story about how her friend Elizabeth's father is marrying a woman who is not Elizabeth's mother and mentioned that her friend Jason was visiting his father over the weekend. Juliette wanted to know whether her father and I are getting married again, despite the fact that we are married to each other. She made no judgment calls and got none from Grandma Claire. Today she watched Sesame Street, then explained to me how families come in all shapes and kinds. She recognized that this is true and she was comfortable with the idea. Yet, when I asked her how she felt about that, she thought for a moment and said that the children will be sad without their mommy and their daddy at home.

Here are the golden rules:

Be brave. You are part of the happy picture. Stay in the picture even when things are, shall we say, tense. Focus on the children and ignore the rest. Keep as much of the happy part alive as possible. The show must go on. Life does.

Have boundaries. Your relationship with your grandchildren is separate from their relationship with their parents. Be consistent in your habits with the children. Do not take sides — at least not out loud. Anything negative you say about either parent will hurt the child. Even if it is a known fact that one parent committed adultery, and the child is a teenager, old enough to understand, it will hurt. It will hurt if such a statement is a mean accusation, and it will hurt even more if it is the truth. To a child, such parental behavior is a kind of betrayal. Don't rub it in.

Especially omit comparisons of the parents. Your grandchild needs to love both parents and have a continuing relationship with each one. They must live with this situation for the rest of their lives. Accentuate the positive ... you.

Avoid triangles. Focus your stories on grandma. Your longing for a different outcome will only add to your grandchild's anxiety. The adjustment is difficult. Don't dig for information or plan miracle cures. Your grandchild needs you to lean on. Create a warm, wonderful world where grandma takes over and no one has to deal with the ugly realities of divorce. Take advantage of your time together to bring them into your world. Let them get to know you — it will be a distraction that will leave you with an even closer relationship.

Custody: a Grandma Is Forever

During the process of separation and divorce, volunteer to join the couple in a child-oriented counseling session with a family therapist. Ask how you can help during this period of transition. Plan a visit around this important event in your family's life. If you cannot, feel free to contact a local family therapist and explore these issues on your own. Focus on how you can be involved with the children in a positive manner.

If you are on good terms with both parents, have a talk with the one getting custody about your future with the children. If your child will not get custody, take the spouse to lunch or have a heart-to-heart on the telephone about your wish to remain in the child's life. Stress how much you love your grandchildren and how important your love is for them. If you are not on wonderful terms with the spouse, request that you be included in the custody agreement with visitation rights that are in "the best interest of" the children. If necessary, call both attorneys directly to discuss this important matter. Try not to get roped into exact schedules — you are more likely to enjoy a full relationship with the children on a more relaxed and timetable. It pays to plan ahead. Don't assume you will be free to see them.

Remarriage

No matter who wins custody, you cannot lose. The grandchildren are yours. Another wedding doesn't change this a bit — it just blesses the children with additional grandparents. They deserve all the love they can get. If you are the "outside" grandma, don't forget that those grandchildren are your blood and you have every right to see them. Help them feel comfortable in the new situation by being a consistent presence. Please don't reject them if your child loses custody and "strangers" now raise them. The grandchildren will feel abandoned by you. Who is being punished here? The children are innocent. So are you.

The remarriage of a parent is overwhelming. Often it means a new house, a new school, and new siblings. New grandparents could tip the bucket. If you have just become the proud new grandparent of your child's new stepchildren, be sensitive to normal feelings of denial that you are, in fact, their grandparent. Be gentle. Treat them the same as your real grandchildren. Odds are you'll have time alone with the original ones when the new ones go visit their grandparents.

Draw your new grandchildren into your traditional activities and create new ones that involve them — whether it's playing checkers or videotaping T-ball practice. Speak to their parents about any problems that may arise. Eventually, the children will settle into a comfortable relationship with you. Then they'll agree that when it comes to grandparents, the more the merrier.

Don't be afraid of the new stepparent. Your grandchildren are likely to be scared enough for everyone. Your respect for a new stepparent will allow him or her to appreciate you. After all, you are helping them out by spending time with the children and making them happy.

Visiting Hours

If possible, see the children away from the custodial parent's influence. Even if your son or daughter has custody, let them know that you are not just part of that package. You are a big part of your grandchildren's heritage, all by yourself. Take the grandchildren out. Invite them to visit your home, even if it means that you must pick them up and bring them there.

The fact that your son or daughter does not have custody doesn't mean he or she must share their sacred visitation period with you. Have your own special time.

Single Parents

When your child is raising your grandchildren single-handedly, your role is even more vital. As four out of five grandmothers agree, "You can catch more flies with honey than with vinegar." In other words, if you're helpful and nice, you'll be a bigger influence than if you're demanding and critical. This holds especially true when dealing with family. Family members are far more sensitive and vulnerable than strangers. After all, you know intimate details of their lives; you're connected forever, whether they like it or not; and you're stepping on their home turf. There may be plenty of pitfalls in his or her methods. Try not be critical or judgmental. Instead, join in and help.

Your Daughter

Studies prove a strong grandmother can serve as a substitute for an absent father. Single women can certainly raise children to be productive and responsible members of society. A partner, however, can reduce the amount of everyday pressure while doubling the amount of available energy. Parental exhaustion might be one reason why it takes two to procreate. This is where you fit in. You can be more than a lifesaver — you can be a fairy godmother! In addition, you have all your experience and wisdom to offer.

The only difference between interference and help is an invitation. Ask how you can help and if you can make some suggestions. Try the approach my mother suggests in therapy: frame your inqueries with "I" statements. Instead of "You're doing that all wrong," try "I know a way that might be easier." Instead of "You should let me do that," try "I'd really enjoy doing that." When you phrase your statements more gently and positively, you avoid making any undue assumptions or accusations toward the other person. Actually, "I" statements are useful tools in everyday communication because they offer an ideal way for people to work together without stepping on each other's toes.

Your Son

If your son is the sole parent, you can be a surrogate mom. Of course, everything is easier if you live nearby. Then you can help with the traditional chores of cooking, shopping, and so forth. Your real value, however, is far more important. While a housekeeper can provide feminine support, her love is not guaranteed. Children need your nurturing. Even if Daddy's girlfriend is playing 'Mommy,' the children need consistent emotional support.

Consider yourself a security blanket — a perfectly soft, warm cotton blanket that your grandchildren snuggle in. You will always be soft; you will always be warm; and you will always be there. You can even be a security blanket for your son.

You know you're a grandma when ...

— you give holiday gifts months before the holidays.

— you keep a box in your closet for forgotten toys.

— you don't mind being spit up on — most of the time.

— you buy a piñata.

18

Getting Involved outside the Family

My grandma just got arrested on TV. You wanna know why?
My grandmother loves us so much that she's gone to jail
to save us from the bomb.
— Edward, age five

Activity Roster

One of the best parts of being a grandmother is connecting with others outside of your family. Not only do you have something in common with trillions of other proud women, but your status as a grandmother can enhance your relationships with everyone else. After all, everyone has a grandmother, whether on Earth or in Heaven.

If your grandchildren are too far away to play with on a regular basis, you can get involved with other children who are nearby. Here are some activities you might enjoy.

• With a giant bubble wand and a bucket of dish soap you could be the "Bubble Lady" at the park. Children love bubbles. Parents might look at you funny at first, but once they know you're a grandma, they'll look forward to seeing you.

• Hospitals and orphanages will welcome your attention. Call the administrator for permission to read stories to individual children or to a group. Many children would appreciate a grandma to talk to, even without a book.

• Check with the library about a Grandparents Reading to Children program. Our local library has one every afternoon from 2:00 to 4:00. Stories are always popular with children — and they contribute to a greater appreciation of reading. Story time also gives parents and caregivers some time to relax and read books without pictures. Reading programs can be informal, where the children pick the books or they can be planned programs that include a related craft activity. One round, tike-sized table in the children's area and a free hour or two every week is all that you need to begin. With prior arrangements, any library would love to have you.

• Public schools can always use volunteers to distribute milk or help on the playground. Many underbudgeted school districts need volunteers to give art and music classes. You don't need a degree or expertise — just enthusiasm about the subject.

• Call the local Girl Scout Council to inquire about being a helper for troop meetings.

• A parks and recreation organization could refer you to a soccer league in need of another coach.

If you live close to your grandchild, you can be involved in their lives in different ways. For example, you may enjoy participating in school or recreational programs:

• Volunteer to be Room Grandma. Schools never have enough Room Parents, and with so many parents working, you'll be doubly appreciated.

• Join the Parent Association and get involved with the lunch program or whatever else interests you.

• Help with the class party on your favorite holiday.

• Supervise or carpool during a school field trip.

• Give a special presentation the students would find interesting. Ask the teacher for suggestions. Depending on the age, you could help kids make peanut butter and jelly sandwiches, an egg carton caterpillar, or a mural.

• Help staff a bake sale.

• Have a grandma booth at the school carnival and charge a nickel per hug!

Being involved with children can be joyous for you as well as the children. Even if you've been a social doyenne all your life, raising money for charities and good causes, there is something unique about offering your time as a grandmother. The difference is love.

Political Rallies

Have you voted since you became a grandmother? If so, I'll bet you thought twice about that school bond issue on the ballot. Maybe you've even started recycling. Rather than burrowing in as your life winds through familiar territory, now is the perfect opportunity to look up and be a part of the world at large. You have a valuable perspective on the world's potential. And goodness knows, you have real, live, huggable reasons to care about what happens in the next month, the next year, and the next century. Your young grandchildren can't vote yet, but you can make sure their interests are represented.

Have you ever seen a grandmother arrested for political activism? How many grandmas lead influential delegations at party conventions? When is the last time you saw a grandmother collecting signatures outside the post office? You would remember, right? Grandmas stand out in every political crowd. The public sympathizes with grandmas, because they represent everything good and loving about families. Consequently, your support of any issue or candidate is quite influential. You don't have to get arrested, but your efforts on the local level of your favorite cause can make a big difference. Your opinion counts — a lot.

Grandmothers for Peace, an international organization based in Elk Grove, California, began in a grandma's living room in 1982 and now holds conferences around the world. Communication between grandmothers of many nations not only provids help on a personal scale, but also echoes in the halls of parliament. Join a local chapter of a group that interests you — or start a new one — to address your concerns about the world your grandchildren are inheriting.

Grandmas can make a difference. The future is yours.

Pep Rallies

Last week a little girl ran up behind a woman at the grocery store. Excited, she called, "Hi, Grandma!" The woman froze in her tracks, turned around, and offered a benign smile. Obviously, the prospect did not thrill her. The girl's mother rushed up to claim her, apologetic. The woman turned on her heel so quickly that the mother's embarrassment turned quickly to disdain. She called after the woman, "She loves her grandma!"

Several days later, a teenager pulled his battered van up behind an older woman at the gas pump. The woman was in control of the Self Serve pump, yet she worked at her own pace. The boy climbed out of his car, paid at the cashier booth, and returned to find the woman slowly screwing her gas cap back on. He glanced at his watch and said, "In this lifetime, grandma!" The woman pulled her shoulders back and turned to him. A proud smile spread across her face.

"Why, thank you, son!"

Being a grandmother isn't about being old, or even passing the torch to younger generations. It's about being loved and revered. It's an existential role in a transient world. Every time you hear the noble title, think of it as a cheer. Hip hip hooray! Be proud.

Class Reunions

When people unite after a long time, peer pressure returns in the form of jealousy and competition. Beauty, wealth, and prestige are important, but they are not everything.

Recently, my mother traveled across the country to her high school reunion in New Jersey. An old beau approached her with his new wife. The wife was younger, of course, and he was working on his second family. He complemented my mother's youth and vitality. My mother smiled at the wife and reminded him that she's still younger than he is. He hugged his wife closer. She pulled out her trump card and showed him pictures of the grandchildren. He dropped his embrace to hold the photographs. "Oh, you're so lucky, Claire," he told her. "I don't have any grandchildren yet."

After the fete for our older daughter's first birthday, we decided to think small for the second. Grandma Claire had a picnic in the park near her house. The only guests, outside of family, were two friends of hers. When they had enough of diapers and birthday cake, the the friends decided to leave. They walked toward their cars and waved goodbye. Unbidden, the baby waved back and blew kisses. My mother, bursting with pride, turned to me and declared, "Now, that's status!"

You know you're a grandma when ...

— your birthday book is always open.

— you buy colored popcorn.

— you look forward to Halloween.

— you send Mother's Day cards to your daughter.

— you smile when you lift up your couch cushion and find broken crayons and mashed cereal.

19

Your Legacy

What history our grandchildren carry within them.
If only D.N.A. could talk.
— Dr. Claire J. Lehr, family therapist

What will your grandchildren remember when they grow up? What toys? What places? What events? What will they think of when they hear the word "grandmother"? Who was there when their parents were not? Who shared their secrets and dreams? What did they learn from you? What image of old age will guide them in later years? What kind of grandparents will they be?

Grandmothers Then and Now

In many vastly different cultures studied by anthropologist Margaret Mead, grandmothers performed a major function. Remember those

National Geographic films? The old women are wise and revered. The lower their breasts sag, the higher on the pedestal they go! Here is the natural order of things. Many animal kingdoms boast a matriarchal society as well. This natural order is based on those most responsible for the continuation of the species.

Although the grandparent/grandchild relationship is universal, outside change has also influenced families, particularly the rise of industrialization. Once families were pulled apart by factory work and the ease of transportation, both European and American societies came to value progress first and foremost. The grandmother, who maintained the humanistic values of the old culture, lost her place on the throne.

The immigrants who came to America embraced progress as the means to a successful future. Your grandmother may have grown up in a close-knit family with many generations living under one roof. When she became a mother, she held on to the ways of the Old World with such a fierce protectiveness that her children couldn't wait to break free. So, at the first scent of independence, your mother escaped. When she had you, she gave you the gift of independence, and you had few expectations of living in the same city, let alone the same house. When she retired, she may have moved even further away, to the sunbelt—Florida or Arizona. When you had children, she embraced modern grandparenting and established the twice-a-year visit. If she stayed for the summer, her friends called her bourgeois.

Today, the vast majority of grandparents have intermittent relationships. You've heard the debate over quality time versus quantity time in regard to career women? With grandparents there is nothing to argue about: a good relationship with grandchildren is determined by the time you spend together. Whether it's weekly play dates or occasional visits backed up by telephone contact, the key work is "together."

You can have the best of both worlds. You don't have to stay in the background. In fact, parents need you now! In this stressful world, providing even such bare necessities as financial security and role modeling can be an overwhelming task for parents . Your greatest purpose is to offer wisdom and love. For parents, children are the entree, for you, they are dessert!

Your Family History

A family has more in common than allergies and skin tone, more than attitudes and habits: it has a shared history, one affected as much by outside influences as by heredity.

What places, people, and politics shaped you? Many cultures

keep their history alive by telling stories around the campfire. Storytelling is not only a way to create legends and tall tales. It is also a way to bequeath your grandchildren a past that will send them confidently into the future.

Children love to hear stories about your childhood. Identifying with you as a child will help them feel especially close to you. Tell them everything you can remember about your family and relatives.

Photographs help a child to visualize your life. They also help to jog your memory and fill in wonderful details. In this transient world, to give children a sense of belonging is very important. A working knowledge of where they came from will help to create a healthy understanding of who they are.

Think of your brain as an Encyclopedia of Special Knowledge. Share all the insightful anecdotes and fascinating facts in your head with your children and your grandchildren. Record your memories with a tape recorder, then pull out the "record" tab on the tape so it cannot be erased. Teach the children about their flesh and blood ancestors and about the places that influenced them — and about you. This personal history is worth more than gold. It is all yours to give them.

Olden Times

Amaze your grandchildren with the wonders of progress. Tell them how you cooked popcorn without a microwave and watched movies without a VCR and listened to the radio before television was invented. They will appreciate modern life.

Help them imagine running free in a daffodil-covered field, walking down the street after dark, and leaving the house without locking the door. They will appreciate "olden" times.

Traditions

Do you remember what you shared with your grandma? Can you share it with your grandchild? The most important tradition to uphold is that of being a loving grandparent.

When my first child was born, my mother took on the role of grandma with a vengeance. I figured her enthusiasm was due to the excitement of her new role and that she would eventually settle back into her old routine, with an extra bubble here and there. After all, she was raised in an untraditional family, which experienced divorce before it was common. Today, she is the ultimate in grandmas, the grandma I wish on every child, and the one I hope to be. Since the day we began talking seriously about this book, tales of her own grandma have come up frequently. And so it hit me. Her grandma was a good example of a grandma, and most likely her grandma's grandma was also a "good" grandma, and hers before that. Continue the tradition in your family—or start a new tradition with you.

My mother remembers her grandma taking her to the duck pond. She was Irish, had long grey hair piled on her head, and was called Nana — the same nickname my children use for Grandma Claire. In the summer, Nana would visit and grandma and grand-daughter would walk together to the duck pond two blocks away. Even today, my mother describes Nana's hair in the same breath as the ducks and swans as she relives those days fifty years ago. Consequently, for her to take my daughter to a duck pond is natural. This duck pond is a little different — a man-made canal in a condo-minium community. Nevertheless, noisy ducks still nest on the grass and scurry for every crumb of bread thrown to the water. Someday, I'll bet Juliette will take her grandchildren to feed the ducks. She'll talk about her Nana's blond hair and how the ducks swam right up to her. Who knows how a duck pond will look by then? Who cares?

Traditions can be — OOPS! Sorry, my husband just burst in. It's 10:00 p.m. and he just got home from work, exhausted. Now he's all flushed with excitement, eyes shining like a young boy's. What hap-pened? He opened the refrigerator and found the jar of old-fashioned orange marmalade I picked up today at a specialty market. Evidently, it's the same brand his "Nanny" used to give him! Here I am, working on a chapter about traditions, and the sight of my husband's grandma's favorite orange marmalade has him conjuring up memories of those special times he shared with her. Obviously, traditions can be quite simple and still have a strong emotional effect.

Almost anything becomes special when it is a family tradition. Visiting Santa, getting a puppy for a birthday present, passing down an antique bracelet, getting a watch at graduation, even teaching a child to bowl can set off a pattern that is more beautiful to behold from a distance. Continue a family legacy — or create a new one.

Personal Connection

Did you ever keep a diary? Do you have any letters from friends that are so special you plan to keep them forever? How many times have you moved and discovered an old box full of treasures from days gone by? Each of these is a personal connection to your past. The understanding you get reading about a difficult period of your life; the giggles that erupt at the sight of your first corsage; the warm glow in your heart as you read your friend's caring missive ... these are all invaluable parts of your life. How about making a personal connection with your grandchild?

A friend of mine, Ralf, recently received a box of his late grandma's effects from Germany. Unfortunately, he never met his grandma. A bond existed, however, to the extent that he named his first child after her. This box was intended for the baby. When he opened it, he felt a more powerful connection to his grandma than he had ever imagined possible. Each item taught him about her and, in turn, about himself. In essence, she has reached out from the past to take her place in the future. Her things will become symbols of the past as well as a part of the present for her namesake great-grandchild.

Write a letter to your grandchildren. Even if you see them every week, you can pen an intimate note for each of them to peruse long after your visits are over. Explain what they mean to you, how you understand them now, and how you envision them to be in the future. Give them your innermost thoughts to savor, to cherish always. Such a letter will be more than a souvenir, it will be a part of their existence. Make that connection.

Helping Your Grandchildren Deal With Death

Death is always traumatic, but a child's first experience with death will set the pace for all those to follow — including yours. Our ten-year-old cat died on Christmas Eve last year, and her death was torturous for all of us. We waited until after Christmas to tell our three-year-old, who adored him. Due to all the excitement with Grandma Claire and Santa and all the gifts, Juliette only asked about the cat once. We told her what had happened the next morning, and she has been talking about death ever since.

Almost every day, she asks another pragmatic question about Heaven. I realize my answers will guide her beliefs for years to come, so I am a little nervous each time the topic arises. I act calm and try to be honest without scaring her. When my husband overheard me one day, he nodded. It was a "that's my story and I'm sticking to it" kind of tacit agreement.

Grandma Claire, having lived a lot longer, is much more relaxed about this. Juliette and she saw a dog and stopped to pet it. Juliette mentioned that she had a cat in Heaven and next year she would like to get a dog. These chats about death are simple and important. Children who cannot discuss death become less free with their emotions. Grandma Claire has taken advantage of Juliette's curiosity by mentioning the possibility of her death someday. She asked Juliette to wear a cheerful yellow dress and carry flowers on that day. Now Juliette can focus on my mother's request rather than on her fear of losing her grandmother. The funeral will feel more comfortable to Juliette as a celebration of life.

The death of loved ones is a horrible loss, but you can make the adjustment period easier. You can give your grandchildren perspective by comparing a family member's passing to how flowers grow and die and how some insects are born and die in the same day. By equating life and death, you can make the event less threatening. This may help to give your grandchildren a warm feeling to keep forever when it is your time. After all, you'll be watching them from Heaven.

Memorabilia

Open the attic to your grandchildren. That old chest full of treasure holds just as much magic for your grandchildren as it does for you. You can explain to the children how you found that lucky rabbit's foot and tell them about the dance when you wore those stained white gloves. Show them the locket your first boyfriend gave you and let them play dress-up with your old mink stole. If your grandchild seems particularly attached to your faded horseback riding ribbon, give it to him outright as a keepsake or put it aside for a special gift later.

Let the children into your life through sharing things that were a part of it. Be a part of their lives by collecting items that are meaningful to all of you and designating them as your time capsule. A squirt gun that won't be missed, a baby tooth, a souvenir program, and a calendar page saved in a shoe box will bring laughs and happy memories a few years from now. Perhaps you'd like to use a coffee can as a time capsule and bury it in the yard. You could create a big event by agreeing on a special date to open the time capsule. Memorabilia is not junk — it's history you can touch!

Create Loving Memories

Most of our earliest memories are emotional ones, whether positive or negative. Memories of grandma will naturally be emotional, as well. My mother remembers her grandma carrying her down the attic stairs during a house fire. Her sister distinctly remembers her grandma not carrying her out of the house. Grandmas can't be everywhere all the time. Be conscious of creating happy memories for your grandchildren not only to remember you by, but also to use as fodder for their own grandparenting styles.

My mother visualizes her grandchild telling her own children stories about their happy times together. When she buys tickets to The Nutcracker, she smiles to herself, imagining her granddaughter recounting their annual trips to the ballet.

Memories of you will make your grandchildren feel loved ... and they will naturally feel love for you.

Happily Ever After

After several months, my friend Donna finally gathered the courage to visit her grandmother's grave. She became very upset when she saw the words "mother" and "wife" carved on the headstone. Immediately, she went to the stone mason and demanded that the title "grandmother" be added. It was more than justice, she felt. It was the highest tribute.

Many people feel that once they have grandchildren, their job on Earth is truly done. They've lived their life, so whatever happens is okay. They can "die happy." (Great-grandchildren are an extra bonus.)

My mother says that since she became a grandma, she's more aware that Heaven is the next step in the life cycle. She also says she doesn't mind, "because now I've got Heaven on Earth."

The Circle of Life

You can give your grandchildren a sense of continuity by reminiscing about the past and dreaming about the future. Remind them that someday, if they are very lucky, they will be grandparents, too.

You know you're a grandma when ...

— the children cry when you leave.

— you stop to smell the roses.

— your favorite bedmate is your granddaughter.

— you feel warm all over.

Resources

Grandmothers for Peace International
Founder & Director: Barbara Wiedner
9444 Medstead Way
Elk Grove, CA 95758
(916) 684-0394 (phone and fax)

**R. F. D. Travel Corporation,
"Grandparents & Grandchildren"**
Contact: Mary Beatty
5201 Johnson Drive
Mission, KS 66205
1-800-365-5359

Today's Young Grandparents Club
Director: Sunie Levin
P.O. Box 11143
Shawnee Mission, KS 66207
(913) 642-8296

Grandmas
are to love

Order Form

Qty.	Title	Author	Order No.	Unit Cost	Total
	Are You Over the Hill?	Dodds, Bill	4265	$6.00	
	10,000 Baby Names	Lansky, Bruce	1210	$3.50	
	35,000+ Baby Names	Lansky, Bruce	1225	$5.95	
	Baby Name Personality Survey	Lansky/Sinrod	1270	$8.00	
	Best Baby Name Book	Lansky, Bruce	1029	$5.00	
	Best Baby Shower Book	Cooke, Courtney	1239	$7.00	
	Best Party Book	Warner, Penny	6089	$8.00	
	Best Wedding Shower	Cooke, Courtney	6059	$7.00	
	If We'd Wanted Quiet/Poems for Parents	Lansky, Bruce	3505	$12.00	
	Funny Side of Parenthood	Lansky, Bruce	4015	$6.00	
	Grandma Knows Best	McBride, Mary	4009	$6.00	
	Grandma's Favorite Photos Brag Book		3109	$8.00	
	Joy of Grandparenting	Holleman/Sherins	3502	$6.00	
	Joy of Marriage	Dodds, M. & B.	3504	$6.00	
	Joy of Parenthood	Blaustone, Jan	3500	$6.00	
				Subtotal	
			Shipping and Handling (see below)		
			MN residents add 6.5% sales tax		
				Total	

YES, please send me the books indicated above. Add $2.00 shipping and handling for the first book and 50¢ for each additional book. Add $2.50 to total for books shipped to Canada. Overseas postage will be billed. Allow up to 4 weeks for delivery. Send check or money order payable to Meadowbrook Press. No cash or C.O.D.'s please. Prices subject to change without notice.
Quantity discounts available upon request.

Send book(s) to:

Name _____ Address _____

City _____ State ____ Zip _____ Phone _____

Payment via:

❑ Check or money order payable to Meadowbrook Press. (No cash or C.O.D.'s please)

Amount enclosed $ _____ ❑ Visa ❑ MasterCard (for orders over $10.00 only.)

Account # _____ Signature _____ Exp. Date _____

A **FREE** Meadowbrook Press catalog is available upon request.

You can also phone us for orders of $10.00 or more at 1-800-338-2232.

Mail to: Meadowbrook Inc., 18318 Minnetonka Blvd., Deephaven, MN 55391

(612) 473-5400   Toll-Free 1-800-338-2232   FAX (612) 475-0736